Winner Takes All

What God Is Still Saying to the Church

J.C. Weeks

WESTBOW®
PRESS
A DIVISION OF THOMAS NELSON
& ZONDERVAN

WestBow Press books may be ordered through booksellers or by contacting:

WestBow Press
A Division of Thomas Nelson & Zondervan
1663 Liberty Drive
Bloomington, IN 47403
www.westbowpress.com
1 (866) 928-1240

ISBN: 978-1-4908-2738-4 (sc)
ISBN: 978-1-4908-2739-1 (hc)
ISBN: 978-1-4908-2737-7 (e)

Library of Congress Control Number: 2014903530

Printed in the United States of America.

WestBow Press rev. date: 2/28/2014

All the world is full of suffering. It is also full of overcoming.
—Helen Keller

To my parents,
Jim and Carolyn Weeks.
Thank you for always showing me
the love of Jesus and
the power of never giving up!

Contents

Acknowledgments

I would like to say thank you to some special friends
whose assistance in writing this book was invaluable.
Darrell and Miriam Hardister
Brian and Kimesha LeFevre
Anthony and Jennifer Beckham

Thank you for the long hours of reading and offering
editorial insights and wisdom. Your knowledge and excellence
in the tips you offered made this venture the best it could be!
May God Bless You!

Preface

At sixty-seven years of age he had always been a strong, healthy, and virile man. He and his wife had worked hard for many years to raise their four children, to provide a loving home, and to instill in them the principles of God's Word. Life had not always been easy or kind to him, and yet through it all he was able to persevere. At times the details of life would become overwhelming as job, family, the roles of being a husband and father, bills, church responsibilities, and weariness pressed in on him, and still he kept going.

Time passed. The children grew up, and he and his wife were beginning to settle into a life of retirement. They were staying busy and active in their church, helping with and loving on their grandchildren, caring for his elderly mother in their home and serving and reaching out to everyone they could. They were enjoying this season in their life, and life was good!

Then August 15, 2012, came, and everything changed.

They say that you never know what a day might bring, and this truth is such a powerful reality. We should all live with this reminder that everything in our lives can change in just a moment, so we should cherish every moment we have. On this seemingly ordinary and uneventful Wednesday, their lives were forever changed.

He had been recovering from an attack of pneumonia and had been in the hospital for a couple days, receiving treatments. On that

Tuesday he was informed that everything was healing well in his lungs and that he would be going home the next day.

Being the type of person who has never really cared for hospitals and doctors, he was excited about the prospect of going home! This little stay in the hospital had been an unwelcome interruption in his schedule of working at home and church, and he was ready to go! His wife was preparing for his homecoming and was happy for his return.

Around midnight he got up out of his hospital bed and fell. As he lay there, unable to move, his roommate heard the fall and called for the nurse to come.

When the nurse arrived, he was able in slurred speech to tell her how he had fallen, and she helped him back into bed. The medical personnel took him for two different CT scans, neither of which revealed anything conclusive. So they decided to just monitor him.

From there things began to deteriorate and go downhill quickly. By 4:00 a.m. that Wednesday he was completely unresponsive. His wife was called, and she immediately rushed to the hospital, unsure of what she would find. When she arrived, she realized that her hopes of picking him up and bringing him home that day would never happen. She didn't know if or when he would ever come home again.

He was taken for an MRI, and she waited. Her children, family, and friends were contacted, and they all rushed to the hospital and waited. It seemed like an eternity.

Finally around 2:00 p.m. on Wednesday, August 15, the family was informed by the neurologist that her husband, who had always been strong and healthy, had suffered a massive ischemic stroke and was still completely unresponsive.

The size and magnitude of his stroke was very significant, as it affected a large portion of the right hemisphere of his brain and also a portion of the brain stem itself.

Rather than going home that day, he was moved to the intensive care unit of the hospital and put on a ventilator. Because of the damage he'd sustained from the stroke, the doctors were unsure if he'd ever be able to breathe on his own again. There was slight movement in his right leg and arm, but the family was told that it was involuntary and not purposeful movement and that they should not get their hopes up about it.

Tests were run. Specialists were consulted. Doctors examined his unresponsive body, and still there was no clear prognosis. The doctors would pessimistically state, "We just have to wait and see," with little or no hope in their words or their eyes!

As the family waited, they took turns staying with him day and night. Twenty-four hours a day and seven days a week, there was someone there who loved him. Scripture reading and prayer were happening in his room continuously.

His family and friends had written Scriptures and inspirational sayings on post-it notes, which were placed all over the walls, bed, medical equipment, and every spare place they could find in his ICU room.

They believed in the healing power of God and would not give up and would not give in. If there was one thing they had learned from his life, it was that when things get too hard, you don't quit and you don't give up!

No matter how devastating the news was they received from the doctors, they would not stop! His family decided early in this process that no matter how small or insignificant, they would celebrate every little victory! They would rejoice over every little bit of progress.

Even though he was completely unresponsive, they spoke to him continuously and interacted with him as though he were there and listening. Their hope was that even if he did not get all of his physical capabilities back, his mind would be strong, his personality and humor would remain the same, and his memory would be intact.

Days passed uncertainly, and progress was slow and minimal. Finally after a week of no real response, he tried very slightly, although unsuccessfully, to open his eyes. The family knew that their fighter was still in there! This process was going to be long, and the progress might be slow; however, they knew he could and would overcome this!

Within two weeks he was breathing on his own and was taken off the ventilator. The doctors were still not hopeful that he would ever recover enough to go home. The family continued to pray and believe. More movement became evident on his right side, and yet still the doctors were not excited about it and said it was not purposeful. But the family knew! Their faith and trust was completely anchored in their Lord, Jesus Christ.

There have been good days when recovery seemed to be moving quickly, and there have been other days when it seemed things were going backward.

For weeks he struggled with the ability to stay awake and alert, and his therapists were concerned because he couldn't maintain consciousness to do therapy. His first therapy session was as simple as him just being able to open his eyes and keep them opened for three seconds.

However, because of his relationship with God and the spirit of an overcomer that lives within him, he has made some great strides. He is out of the hospital and in a rehabilitation center. God has blessed him with three *great* therapists (physical, occupational, and speech) who have challenged him.

Miracle after miracle is taking place in him, but it has come with a price! One day during his physical therapy he told his wife and his therapist through his mumbled and slow words, "This is really hard."

His wife lovingly looked at him and said, "I know it is, but you can do this."

His therapist told him, "This is the hardest thing you will ever do in your life. But you can do it, and we will do it together."

And he is doing it! I know this because this man and his wife are my parents, Jim and Carolyn Weeks.

All of my life I have watched them take everything that has come their way and deal with it victoriously. Through the good, the bad, and the worse, the heart of a godly warrior has been easily evident in them. I am so thankful to have learned what overcoming can mean to me by watching their lives!

I've seen my dad's struggle to overcome his understanding of what happened to him. I've been a witness to the hardships he has gone through as he tries to get parts of his body that used to function easily to even move in the slightest way now. I've recognized his frustration with not being able to communicate the way he always did. This man who had always been so strong and independent has swallowed a bitter pill to become so vulnerable and dependent on others for even the simplest things.

I have watched my mom stay by his side all day long every day through these last few months, at times not knowing if he would survive. And if he did, would he ever be the same? I've identified with the fear and worry she felt. I have seen the uncertainty and weariness that at times has filled her eyes and wondered how this woman can endure these things and continue to be filled with such strength and faith.

My dad still has a long way to go, but this strong man is winning the battle every day! Some days his healing and victory comes through intense physical therapy, and other days the best healing and victory comes through simply resting.

One of the lessons I have learned through this about overcoming is that sometimes we must fight, struggle, and work hard, and then sometimes we just need to rest.

One day shortly after dad went into rehab and was for the most part stable but still primarily unresponsive, his therapist came in and shared something with my mom that was an incredible encouragement. This therapist, who had never said anything about being a Christian or having faith in God, said to my mom, "I don't normally have dreams when I sleep at night, and when I do, I *never* dream about my patients. But last night I had a dream about your husband. I dreamed that he was standing up and walking the hallways of this rehab center and talking with everyone he passed in the hallway."

For a family who was looking at a man we were uncertain would ever be able to do anything again, this was a fresh word from God that served to further solidify our faith in the Great Physician.

My parents are people who are deeply in love with each other and even more deeply in love with Jesus Christ! Day by day, hour by hour, moment by moment, and second by second, we are overcoming this event that has shaken our family. The spirit that God has placed in my dad is driving him to make a full recovery, and that is what we are believing for.

By Thanksgiving 2012 the man the doctors weren't even sure was going to survive was able to go home for the day for Thanksgiving dinner with his family around a table filled with turkey and all kinds of food. Even though he still could not eat solid foods his family were giving God thanks for all He had done!

This is what I think of when I think of overcoming. But what does it mean to you? This principle of being victorious goes even beyond physical infirmities. There are spiritual, mental, emotional, and physical barriers that at times we must break through.

Introduction

What does it mean to *overcome*? How can I be an *overcomer*? When will I finally get past all the struggles, temptations, difficulties, and addictions I face every day? How will I ever surmount the seemingly insurmountable things that have kept me from walking the walk of an overcomer?

The ability to overcome problems and adversity is a crucial ingredient of our character that every one of us must work to acquire. It's not something that comes easy and often requires a price of sacrifice.

We want to do better. We long to have full, abundant, and successful lives, but we keep bumping into this hurdle that we can't seem to get over. We find ourselves tripping and falling on our faces every time we try to jump over it. If we try to go around it, there is another one beside it that defies us! We feel lost in this vicious cycle of inadequate successes and ultimately bigger failures. We want to know the invigoration and joy of being free from this vortex of defeat. We see others who have risen above situations and obstacles in their lives and have experienced the hope and happiness of triumph... so why can't we?

That's a good question, "Why can't I?" you may ask. There are many self-help books and social programs doing great things in our society, but let me ask you this: When you think about "the one who overcomes," what comes to your mind? What do you envision when you hear those words?

Do you visualize the victories of skilled warriors on the field of battle? Do you think of Olympic athletes who go through rigorous training and master so many obstacles to excel at their sport? Do you consider the addicts who have successfully come out on the other side of their addictions? Or maybe your mind goes to the single parent who has come through a difficult time and is now strong and doing well.

We look at these examples and say, "I can never do that. I have tried and tried and always failed."

While we are walking through the everydayness of our lives, it is easy to become discouraged and lose sight of the ultimate goal. We get tunnel vision and become shortsighted, and little victories go unnoticed. We end up nearsighted by focusing only on what is happening right now, and we make choices based on how we feel in this moment rather than having vision to see how choices today can affect victories tomorrow.

We were not placed on this earth just to maintain and get by however we can; God has a much deeper meaning and a higher calling for our lives. No matter what our history, experiences, or current situations, God has a plan for us.

Nikao (nik-ah'-o) is the Greek word for overcome. (It is where we get our word Nike.) And this word means to conquer, to subdue (literally or figuratively), to overcome, to prevail, to get the victory (*Biblesoft's New Exhaustive Strong's Numbers and Concordance with Expanded Greek-Hebrew Dictionary* 1994).

We live in a world where it is much easier to compromise than to conquer. Little things that could bring great victories in our lives are neglected or back-burnered to deal with more pressing issues.

In the hunt for a victorious life, we find ourselves chasing rabbits down little trails, and we never seem to find the illusive big game of victory we desire! We get caught up in the problems and stresses of each day and miss out on the greater spectrum of what it means to be an overcomer.

We strap on our helmet and run headlong into the wall that is standing in our way, thinking that this time we will finally knock it over, only to regain consciousness and realize the wall is still there and we are lying on the ground flat on our backs. As a result, what do we do? We straighten our helmet, step back a little farther than last time to give us a better running start, and hit the wall again! If you are like me, after you do this hundreds of times, you finally acquiesce and rationalize that maybe the wall is not really all that bad right where it is.

In the seemingly frazzled and battered days of our lives, we pray, "God help me to just *survive* today," with little or no thought of what it could mean in our lives to live *victorious* today.

What could it mean for your life if you were to get out of the survivor mentality and begin living the abundant life Jesus speaks of in John 10:10?

There is a place of victory and abundance God has declared and destined for our lives. We must be careful not to miss finding this place because everything else in life has crowded in around us and obscured us from the spiritual vision to see it!

We must understand that overcoming is more a daily mind-set than it is a final destination. We can see in the distance the rewards of overcoming and being victorious, and we say "That is where I want to be." However, those words don't always seem to be enough to motivate us and help us in the day-to-day struggle.

When my family and I travel, I know where our final destination is, and my agenda is to get there as quickly as possible. It would be nice to have a time machine that could simply transport us from one geographical location to the next within seconds, but unfortunately that is not how the journey plays out.

We have to get in the car and drive one mile at a time until we finally reach our destination. Throughout the drive we endure all the setbacks of bathroom stops and lunch breaks that seem to distract us, tick away the minutes, and keep us from reaching our destination! If we were to give up halfway through the journey because it is taking too long and turn around to head back, we would never reach the goal of seeing our family or enjoying our vacation!

This same concept applies to our lives. The Bible emphasizes to us in Romans 12:2 that we must be "transformed by the renewing of our minds." We must change our mind-set about overcoming like the recovering drug addict or alcoholic does and see that our ultimate victory is in the daily showing up for the battle.

We need to set our sights on winning each battle one second, one minute, one hour, or one day at a time. Each day we need to purpose in our hearts that this is going to be a day of victory for me. We must abandon defeatist attitudes and excuses that would keep us from being victorious.. It is a daily process. We must overcome in the little things to be able to overcome in the bigger things. On my trip I will never reach mile marker #638 if I don't first pass by mile marker #1.

I'm reminded of a boy named David whose story is found in the Old Testament. He didn't start out by toppling a giant. No! He started in the field, watching over sheep and defending them against both small and large predators. He knew his sheep, and he knew the other beasts that would try to attack his flock. He knew the damage and destruction that could happen if he compromised because a bear seemed too big or a lion appeared too ferocious. He would lose everything if he didn't show up for the battle.

Just because we kill a lion today doesn't mean there won't be another one tomorrow. Even so, we must do what needs to be done each day to secure that day's victory because troubles can show up at any time, and we must be ready!

It wasn't until after David defeated the lion and the bear that he stood up and defied the giant standing in his way. Goliath came into the "flock of Jehovah" as a predator, and David would just not stand for Goliath's threat to become a reality.

While the king and the other great warriors trembled in their armor, David put on the garment of an overcomer and stood unwavering. He had already been victorious before as the caretaker of his father's sheep, and he wasn't afraid of the one who would come against his heavenly Father's sheep.

David walked past all those who said he couldn't do it. He ignored those who said he was too young. He didn't even pay attention to the fact that the armor was too big for him. The fear that stopped others would not stop him.

All David knew was that an uncircumcised giant (someone not of the promise of God) was standing in the way of God's plan and God's people and that this giant must fall! He quickly retrieved his slingshot and with a few stones brought that giant down.

A slingshot may not have been a great instrument of war or a weapon of mass destruction, but even something small things in the hands of someone anointed by the Spirit of God is powerful. The people who have their eyes set on victory are greater than the most lethal weapon known to man!

We must be careful to win in the small things, for this will give us faith and strength for the bigger giants.

As a child must first learn addition and subtraction before he or she can eventually learn algebra, so we must first learn to seek out conquest in the little issues of our lives before we can tackle the big ones!

Throughout Scripture we are reminded to be overcomers and to live in victory. Consider the following passages: "You, dear children, are from God and have overcome them, because the one who is in you is greater than the one who is in the world" (1 John 4:4 NIV). "Do not be overcome by evil, but overcome evil with good." (Romans 12:21 NKJV) "He replied, 'I saw Satan fall like lightning from heaven. I have given you authority to trample on snakes and scorpions and to overcome all the power of the enemy; nothing will harm you'" (Luke 10:18–19 NIV).

My desire in this book is to walk us through Revelation 2–3 to discover, with greater clarity and understanding through the Spirit of God, what He is saying to the church today. These letters written to the seven churches of Revelation hold some powerful principles for us, even in our twenty-first-century society, about overcoming, the rewards of the overcomer, and what the Spirit of God is speaking to the body of Christ in this postmodern age.

I hope to show how important it is that we pursue the life of victory. *Get ready because the winner takes all!*

CHAPTER 1

Ready for a Revelation!

Let's begin by looking at the writer of the Revelation. It is widely accepted that this John, who was exiled to the Isle of Patmos, is the same one who was the disciple and apostle of Jesus Christ.

He is also known as John the Beloved, who was resting on Jesus during the Last Supper before Christ's crucifixion. He had followed Christ and loved Him with all his heart. He had a passion for the things of Christ that seemed different than the other disciples because when the others were running for their lives during the time of Christ's crucifixion, John was standing at the cross with Mary, the mother of Jesus.

As we come to this time of Revelation in John's life, we realize that at this moment John had every right to feel defeated. No one could have blamed him if he had felt overwhelmed and beaten down because of the place where life had taken him.

He had made all the right choices and yet found himself destitute and abandoned because of his faith in Jesus Christ. He had given his whole life to the work of God and the propagation of the gospel. His peers in ministry had been executed for the cause of Christ. He had suffered many personal persecutions and now found himself alone on an island.

This man could have wondered why God had brought him to this place. Serious issues of depression could have overtaken him because he had devoted his whole life to the cause of the gospel and now found himself alone, mistreated, and seemingly defeated. However, there was something greater at work here in John's life than just where he found himself in that instant.

If we could wrap our minds around that in our walk with God, how much different would our perspective of the difficulties we are facing right now in life be? There is something greater that God is working on in us than just what we are going through at this moment.

Under the inspiration of the Holy Spirit in writing to Ephesus, John first mentions his life-changing encounter with Jesus Christ. What was just another seemingly ordinary day would turn out to be one of the most incredibly powerful and intimate days of his life with the Lord.

While Christ was walking with His disciples on the earth, they spent a lot of time together. John had watched Jesus do ministry, miracles, and the supernatural. Their relationship was very close, and John was totally sold on His Lord and Savior.

The miracles that he had watched Christ do were amazing. The time he had spent with Jesus at the last supper was intimate. The prayer with the Lord in the garden of Gethsemane was challenging. Watching Christ die a brutal death on a cross was agonizing. Finding that Jesus had risen on the third day was exhilarating and inspiring.

However, none of that could have prepared him for this day in the presence of Jesus Christ and the Revelation that was waiting to be imparted to him.

In Revelation 1:10, John said, "I was in the spirit on the Lord's Day." John, the disciple and apostle, possibly the last remaining of the original twelve, found himself displaced on the Isle of Patmos, a small island in the Aegean Sea.

Can you for just a moment put yourself in John's shoes? Maybe you can relate to John because you feel that life has taken you to some remote place physically or spiritually, a place you never imagined yourself going.

You may feel as though you have lost everything, or if not everything, at least enough that you are beginning to wonder what God is doing to you.

John was human just like us. Could it be he also had his moments of not understanding what God was doing? Perhaps.

As we take a closer look at this amazing man, we get some insights into the life of someone who has truly overcome and someone who is truly in love with his Savior. John wasn't sitting around and complaining to himself about his predicament. We don't find him moping around the island, wondering if God had forsaken him in the middle of this difficult time in his life. There was no whining and bellyaching to God coming from his lips. He wasn't even trying to find a way off the island or trying to get out of his predicament.

We find him "in the Spirit on the Lord's Day." How amazing is that?

He might have been singing praises or hymns. He could have been testifying to the rocks and dirt and recounting the blessings of God or reciting psalms he had memorized.

We don't know for sure what he was doing, but we do know he was in the spirit on the Lord's day and the presence of God was shown to him in a powerful way. If we could only get this same attitude in us to look beyond the triviality of our current situation and imagine the greater things God has in store for us.

John was right where he needed to be in order to see what God wanted to reveal to him!

Is it possible that the situations of your life have simply placed you in the position you need to be in for you to hear what God wants to speak to you? It may not seem like the easiest or most comfortable or most convenient place to be, but perhaps it is precisely where you need to be to receive your revelation from the Lord.

God hasn't promised that life would always be an easy ride or a garden of flowers in which to stroll. Sometimes it is imperative for Him to get us away from everything and on our own Isle of Patmos in order to get our attention. When He does, we have to be ready to listen for His voice.

We might assume that John was alone on that island, but if we could pull back the curtain of the natural and peek into the supernatural, we would discover that he wasn't alone at all. The Father, the Son, and the Holy Spirit were there with him.

He was "in the Spirit on the Lord's Day" and found himself transported beyond his current geographical location to a place of holy ground. Past all the struggles of being on the island and the potential disappointments about where life had taken him, he found himself in the presence the Almighty! He was brought into the throne room of the King of Kings.

He saw beyond the temporary issues of life to see through the eyes of the Spirit what was truly surrounding him. He didn't complain. He worshipped. He didn't whine. He worshipped. He didn't blame God. He worshipped, and the Spirit of the Lord was present. He overcame his situations and came into the presence of God.

We can so easily get sidetracked by the fleeting debris that life seems to blow into our lives (problems, difficult relationships, financial woes, crazy drama, and life in general not working out as we had anticipated) that we miss the true reality of why God has us where we are. It is a trap of the Enemy to be so consumed with what is happening *to* us that we miss seeing what God wants to do *in* us!

When life throws us curve balls, we don't need to throw the bat down and give up. We need to worship.

When things don't work out the way we had planned, we need to trust God to lead us and we must worship.

When that familiar temptation comes knocking at our door *again*, we must flee from it, come close to God, and worship.

When a relationship hasn't gone as we expected and we feel as if the world has turned its back on us, we must remember that He is always with us, and we must worship.

When we pray and don't seem to get an answer, we must remind ourselves that God is listening and that He will answer at just the right time. We must have faith, and we must worship!

Even if the journey of life takes us down unfamiliar roads and there are detours along the way we didn't expect, we must keep following and worshipping Him. We know and are fully persuaded that our God directs the steps of His children. So it is no mere coincidence that John found himself on this island. He was simply following the plan God had laid out for his life. It is also no coincidence that you find yourself where you are. You are simply where God needs you to be in order to speak into your life!

Will you have enough trust in God to say, "Lord, wherever You lead me, I will follow You. I will trust You. I will worship You!"?

We have an amazing portal into this revelation because John was an overcomer and he worshipped. So let's take a look at a segment of what he saw and heard to uncover what the Spirit is still saying to the church as a whole and to each of us individually.

CHAPTER 2

Falling in Love... Again!
Church of Ephesus

To the angel of the church of Ephesus write,
"These things says He who holds the seven stars in His right hand,
who walks in the midst of the seven golden lampstands: 'I know your
works, your labor, your patience, and that you cannot bear those
who are evil. And you have tested those who say they are apostles
and are not, and have found them liars; and you have persevered
and have patience, and have labored for My name's sake and have
not become weary. Nevertheless I have this against you, that you
have left your first love. Remember therefore from where you have
fallen; repent and do the first works, or else I will come to you
quickly and remove your lampstand from its place—unless you
repent. But this you have, that you hate the deeds of the Nicolaitans,
which I also hate. He who has an ear, let him hear what the Spirit
says to the churches. To him who overcomes I will give to eat from
the tree of life, which is in the midst of the Paradise of God.'"

—Revelation 2:1–7 (NKJV)

The church of Ephesus was perhaps not just a single congregation of people but a representation of the whole Body of Christ in the city! What is immediately apparent in this Scripture is that the church in Ephesus seemed to be doing a lot of good things. They seemed to be a church on the move. They were working hard for the kingdom.

Great strides were being made for the gospel in this church. A vigorous stance against sin was evident in this body of believers. The church at Ephesus was patiently enduring the persecution they faced. They were showing discernment and wisdom in exposing those who would come in and deceive the believers.

These are all great things. So what was wrong?

It would seem odd that a church making such an impact could still find themselves displeasing to God. Could it be that the issue of this church was not a sin of commission (actively committing sin) but rather a sin of omission (omitting or leaving out something that is crucial)?

Have you ever found yourself guilty of that? You may think that just because you are not intentionally living a lifestyle of sin, then you must be okay. Are there things you should be doing and are not? Have you neglected reading and studying the Word of God in your life? Are you a person of prayer and fellowship with God? Is the voice of the Holy Spirit a voice to which you respond immediately and intentionally?

Life can be so fast-paced that we find ourselves without the time or energy to do some of the things we must do if we are going to see victory.

We cannot neglect important spiritual principles in our lives and then wonder why we always feel defeated. It would be like walking into a room with your hands over your eyes and asking, "Why is it dark in here?"

No matter how hard the church of Ephesus could work or how many ministries they could be involved in or how many lies they could expose for the sake of the truth, these things could not sustain their first love.

All these are wonderful things and are to be commended, but they cannot replace a vibrant, passionate love relationship with the Savior.

When you are truly in love with someone, everything else takes a backseat to that relationship. This intimacy becomes the focal point of your life, and everything else is simply peripheral. This church needed to return to their first love and fall in love with Jesus all over again!

By the same token, we also can do a lot of good works and even strive to reach many for the cause of Christ, but if in the process of working in the kingdom, we neglect the things which are central to our relationship with Jesus, we can easily find ourselves distanced from our first love in Him.

Long-distance relationships can be very difficult and rarely work out for good. So why would we try to carry on a long-distance relationship with the one who gave everything for us so that we could draw near to Him?

We can get so busy and so caught up doing good things that we don't have time for the necessary things. Time can steal the fervor of our fellowship with Him. Concerns of life can wrap around our hearts and become all-consuming until we are languished and there is no time or energy left in our day to simply sit with Him, commune with Him, and bask in His love for us.

We make sure we find time to invest in the people and things we truly love! If we love our families, we will show them by spending time with them every day, speaking blessing to them, pouring into them, and telling them how much we love them. If certain people love to fish, they will reschedule other important things on their calendar in order to go fishing. How much more important is it for us to do the same with our Creator?

However, more often than not, it feels as if our daily personal devotions are only fit into each day if we can find a little bit of time in our busy lives. If we pray at all, our daily prayer becomes nothing more than a few lethargic sentences that we feel obligated to offer and that are void of any true affection or fervency. These hurried prayers become simply our wish list of blessings as if God is nothing more than our sugar daddy in the sky. Our reading and study of God's Word is diminished to Sunday only when the minister asks us to turn to his text for the morning, if we even took the time to bring our Bible to church.

We find ourselves too frazzled and too stressed to truly come into the throne room and presence of God just to sit at His feet and hear His voice. Too many other things are happening that don't allow us to "lie down in green pastures, or be led beside the still waters or to have our souls restored by the Shepherd" (Psalm 23:2-3).

Our minds are distracted and racing. We've got to go, go, go and do, do, do. We no longer have time for those moments alone with Him to be refreshed, restored, and rejuvenated.

We become like Martha from the story in Luke 10:38-42, who was frantically running around, working, serving, and asking Jesus for things rather than being like her sister, Mary, who chose better and was content to just sit at Jesus' feet, hear His words, and be in His presence. Both of these women were friends with Jesus and loved Him, but Martha's actions were motivated by obligation while Mary's flowed from relationship.

The human heart can be so fickle when it comes to our relationships, and if we are not careful, this can flow into our fellowship with God!

No matter how much we can serve or how many people we may win to Christ (which we should definitely be doing because there is truly a harvest to reap), there is considerable danger in getting too caught up in working *for* Him that we ourselves end up having no relationship *with* Him.

In the process of serving, we must not neglect relationship. What will it profit a man if he gains the whole world and loses his own soul? Or what will a man give in exchange for his soul? (Mark 8:36-37).

There is urgency in what John wrote to the church in Ephesus. The Spirit was saying to the church, "Unless you wake up and repent, there will be severe consequences." The fact that the church had walked away from their first love, their relationship with Christ, the whole reason they were supposed to be doing what they were doing, had caused it to become sin to them. Whenever there is sin, there must also be repentance.

The church at Ephesus could not just say, "Oh well, we're only human. We will try to do better." No! They had to *repent!*

It wasn't about just doing more stuff. Nor was it about being involved in more ministries. True repentance requires humility and sincerity in turning away from the things that have kept them and us from Christ.

We can't say, "I'm sorry, Lord," and then get up from the altar of repentance and not change anything about the way we live our lives. True repentance will bring change. A transformation in our intentions, actions, and words must always follow repentance. Otherwise it becomes an unacceptable offering to the Lord.

The Spirit spoke to the members of the church at Ephesus and told them that if they did not repent and do their first works again, He would come quickly and remove their lamp stand from them.

What in the world does that mean?

The golden lamp stand (or menorah) in the history of Israel has a wealth of significance attached to it. The lamp stand is a lamp with a base, a shaft, and six branches that flow out of the shaft.

At the top of the shaft and six branches were decorative cups in the shape of almond blossoms that were fueled and kept lit by oil (representing the presence and anointing of the Holy Spirit).

If you look at the articles contained in the temple, the golden lamp stand was located in the Holy Place. It was the only source of light in the Holy Place and illuminated the Holy Place so the priests could perform their ministries.

This golden lamp stand was to shine all the time. It was never to be extinguished to serve as a reminder to the people that God was always with them. It was the responsibility of the priests to care for the lamp stand twice a day to make sure it continued to burn brightly.

The seven golden lamp stands mentioned in Revelation 2:1 refer to the seven churches to whom the Spirit is speaking. Jesus is walking in the midst of those seven lamp stands, meaning His presence, His anointing, and His Spirit is in those churches.

As the light of the world, He is leading them and anointing them to fulfill the purpose of their calling. Fueled by His presence and His Spirit, these churches were to go into the darkness of their world and be the light of Jesus. They were to expel darkness and shine forth into the world like the morning sun chases away the night.

But how could they shine if their light was eclipsed by sin in their lives? Their absence of a love for Jesus had become sin to them, and darkness was blinding them.

They were oblivious to the fact that their works had consumed them and robbed them of the real purposes of their hearts. God sent Jesus Christ to restore His relationship with His creation. When this relationship is not maintained by those who claim the name of Christ, it is displeasing to the heart of God.

Have you ever given gifts to people you love and thought the presents were something they really wanted only to discover they put the items on the shelf or in storage somewhere and never used them? Or maybe they regifted the gifts rather than using them. How did that make you feel?

Now think about this: God loves us and gave us the best gift we could ever expect to receive, and too often this gift is placed on the shelf or in an obscure storage area within our hearts and lives and never really received or used. I wonder how that makes God feel.

Where there is sin, the Spirit of the Lord will not abide. His holiness does not permit Him to allow sin to go unchecked in the lives of those who proclaim His name!

If there was no repentance in the church at Ephesus, then judgment would be swift and severe. He would remove His presence and His Spirit, and this church would be no more.

In other words, if they did not repent, they would be removed from the Body of Christ. Being cut off, nothing they did would be effective or fruitful. That may seem a little harsh, given they were accomplishing great things for the kingdom, but that is the importance God places on His relationship with us through His Son.

Jesus made reference to this in John 15:5–10 (NKJV) when He said,

I am the Vine, you are the branches. He who abides in Me, and I in him, bears much fruit; for without Me you can do nothing. If anyone does not abide in Me, he is cast out as a branch and is withered; and they gather them and throw them into the fire, and they are burned. If you abide in Me, and My words abide in you, you will ask what you desire, and it shall be done for you. By this My Father is glorified, that you bear much fruit; so you will be My disciples. As the Father loved Me, I also have loved you; abide in My love. If you keep My commandments, you will abide in My love, just as I have kept My Father's commandments and abide in His love.

God loves us so much that He gave everything He could to be reconciled to us and have an ongoing, daily relationship and fellowship with us. The Father did not send Jesus into this world and to the cross just so we could build big churches, have lots of ministries taking place, or constantly have entertaining activities happening in the church.

He sent His Son for a *personal love relationship*. For His creation to willingly love Him is exactly what His heart desires. He longs for us to abide in His love. If busyness, activities, or stress steal that time and communion, it breaks the heart of God. He is jealous for us and yearns for us to be in His presence.

In the great love story that is the Song of Solomon, armed with an understanding that this is symbolic of God (and Christ's) love for the church, listen to how it is described in Solomon 8:6–7(NKJV), "Set me as a seal upon your heart, As a seal upon your arm; For love is as strong as death, Jealousy as cruel as the grave; Its flames are flames of fire, A most vehement flame. Many waters cannot quench this love, Nor can the floods drown it."

His love for us is vast and immeasurable. There is nothing that can quench His love for us or take it away from us. He loved us even when we were unlovable and did not love Him.

John 3:16 (NKJV) states, "For God so loved the world that He gave His only begotten Son that whoever believes in Him should not perish but have everlasting life."

God's first love was for you! He is passionate about you, and that devotion motivated Him to give the only gift that could bring the results He desired—His Son, Jesus Christ!

He has never walked away from or substituted anything for His first love—*you!* He is constantly trying to draw you near to a place of surrender and commitment. He continuously beckons for you to come away with Him. He wants you to forget about all the things in life that rob you of your time together with Him. He longs for you to give Him your undivided attention. But so many times we are too busy running around like the proverbial chickens with our heads cut off, trying to do more and be more that we miss those moments when He is calling us to come near and just be with Him.

The relevance of this for the church today is sobering. We live in a fast-paced, microwaved society that values immediate gratification. We scurry around, not realizing the cares of this life or the stresses we are under. At times even the ministries we are involved in can begin to slowly steal our passion for Christ and our life.

Raising a family, transporting kids to school and sporting events, going to church two to three times a week, working full-time jobs, cooking dinner, cleaning the house—and the list could go on—all delivers us to a place where, even if we have the aspiration to pursue God, we do not have the energy or the time for the follow through.

How sad it is when we can become so sidetracked by everything we think we need to do and be that we miss out on the daily and eternal blessings of fellowship and growth in the one who gave so much for a relationship with us!

Please don't misunderstand me. I am not against ministries, activities, building churches, or working for the kingdom, for faith without works is dead. We *must* be about the Father's business.

That being said, let me also say that it doesn't matter how many Sunday school classes you teach or sermons you prepare and preach, how effectively you can lead praise and worship, or how many strangers you can witness to on the street. If you are not daily growing in a passionate love relationship with the Savior, then you have nothing.

If you don't have the time to be refreshed and renewed in Him each day, then you are just doing busy work and will eventually be ineffective.

In some ways, it is a lot like a cell phone. If the phone is not periodically set aside and charged, eventually the battery will die, and no matter how awesome the phone may look or how smart the phone may be when fully charged, it will be absolutely no good to anyone if the battery is dead. The phone cannot fulfill its purpose.

You can go through the motions and sway people with your talents and giftedness. People can perceive you to be the most spiritual person they know, but it is not the perception of others or the talent you may possess that will ensure and preserve your love for God!

People can say they love God every single day of their lives, but the one who knows the hearts and thoughts of His creation knows whether it is true love or simply lip service.

God will only allow us to carry on in this arena of lost love for so long before He will come and remove the lamp stand (His Spirit, His anointing, and His glory) from our lives and our churches.

God help us to not pour ourselves into futile, temporary things but to think of the greater eternal cause! God teaches us to sincerely echo the psalmist David's words when he prayed, "Create in me a clean heart, O God, and renew a steadfast spirit within me. Do not cast me away from Your presence, and do not take Your Holy Spirit from me" (Psalm 51:10–11 NKJV).

God loves you. God desires you. God's heart longs for you. No matter how close you are to Him right now or how far away you have run from Him, His love for you never changes. His love is seeking you out. His love is stalking you everywhere you go!

This is why He gave the opportunity to the church in Ephesus to repent and return. He loved them and wanted to bring them back to their first love!

If His plan was to just remove the lamp stand and strip them of His presence to teach them a lesson, He could have done that, but this wasn't the result He hoped for.

He gave them the chance to return and do their first works again. What were their first works? They were falling in love with Jesus and accepting and abiding in His love.

My friend, God is calling us back. It is not always easy to overcome the mentality, especially in a world that justifies any type of lifestyle and says, "Oh, I'm all right. I'm doing okay. I'm happy with what I am doing and where I am in life."

But this distraction and casual nature about our relationship with Christ will have severe consequences if we do not carefully guard against it. No matter how we may justify our lives or activities or how we feel we measure up when compared to other people, God sees the true condition of our hearts, and He knows what we do and why we do it!

Consider the apostle Peter. He walked with Christ in ministry for three years. He had heard the teachings of Jesus. As he watched, the sick were healed by Jesus' touch, and the demon possessed people were delivered.

He was witness to the dead being raised to life, and Peter had walked on top of the water to the arms of Jesus. He was the man who had delivered the message of the Father when he proclaimed to Jesus, "You are the Christ, the Son of the living God."

From all appearances, Peter's relationship with Jesus should have been so tight that even death itself could not alter it. Yet during the arrest and trial of Jesus, when the crunch time of Calvary was on, Peter allowed the distraction of what others perceived him to be and his fear of the future to distort his vision and passion for Jesus. This drove him to a three-time denial of even knowing Christ. He left his first love. He completely walked away from it and acted as though he didn't even know Jesus.

Perhaps this is why it is recorded in John 21:15–17 that after His resurrection, Jesus asked Peter three times, "Do you love Me?"

Jesus was calling him back to his first love. He was reminding Peter of the love he must have in order to do the work that had been set before him. Peter had denied Jesus three times, and three times Jesus called him back to his first love.

It was out of Peter's love for the Savior that he would go on to effectively fulfill his life's calling. Jesus wasn't reprimanding Peter or trying to make him feel guilty. Jesus loved Peter and wanted God's best in his life, and the only way that could happen was for Peter to be refocused on what was truly important.

Often we can set our eyes on what seems immediate and critical rather than on what is truly necessary and important.

Distraction takes our focus, our time, and our energy from where it should be and puts it on temporary and nonessential things rather than on eternal ones.

Whether the distraction that has caused you to leave your first love is sin, addiction, hurt, resentment, anger, unforgiveness, workload, ministry cares, fear, anxiety, worry, stress, family, friends, or any other thing, God wants you back!

He is missing the sweet fellowship and communion you used to share. He is calling you. He is wooing you. He desires those alone times with you. He wants you to lay your head on His chest and hear His heartbeat and share His Spirit. You must make a choice to take your eyes off the distraction, repent, and turn to Him.

It is said that the first step to recovery is admitting there is a problem. We can't find that first love again until we recognize we have lost it and repent.

Many may read this and say to themselves, "I haven't lost my first love. I still love Jesus," to which I respond, "Look at your life and look at your schedule and see where your priorities really are. Don't gloss over the issue by thinking that just because you were raised in the church and have always been a good person and you do and say the right things, you really love Jesus. If He is not the center of your life, the first thing you think of in the morning, the one you fellowship with throughout the day, and the last one you speak to at night, then perhaps there is a loss of love in your life."

When we fall in love with someone we want to spend every moment we can with him or her. We want to go where that person goes, do what he or she does, and listen to what our love says.

When we truly love Christ, we won't be embarrassed for Him to go where we go. We won't feel guilty for Him to watch what we watch on television. We won't be ashamed for Him to hear our conversations with others throughout the day.

We must fall in love with Jesus all over again! We must run back to that first love just like the prodigal son ran back to his father's arms and be overwhelmed with His love for us!

The Scripture says there is a reward for those who recognize they have fallen and lost their first love and then repent and come back to Him. There is reward for those who overcome the attitude of complacency and return to the excitement and passion that they first had in their love for Christ.

Adam and Eve loved walking with God in the garden of Eden. Their times of fellowship with Him in the cool of the evening were sweetly desired. They were deeply in love with their Creator as He was in love with them, but the voice of distraction called to them. When Adam and Eve made the choice to eat of the Tree of the Knowledge of Good and Evil, the one thing in the garden God had strictly forbidden, they immediately found themselves wandering the landscape of lost love. Something was different.

Their love and desire for the presence of God was turned into fear and hiding. Although they had been naked from the day of their creation and it had never been an issue before now, they were ashamed and didn't want Him to look upon their nakedness.

They wanted to hide from Him rather than hug Him! The thought of being with Him no longer stirred their hearts with excitement but filled them with trepidation.

Because of their disobedience, they were banished from the garden and now would never know the unspeakable joy of partaking of the Tree of Life. It seemed that all hope was lost and that there was no way back to the love of God. There was no way of reentering the garden because it was sealed off with a flaming sword and protected by angelic beings.

As a result, humanity was utterly and completely lost! Adam and Eve had relinquished their rights to the presence of God and had plunged all of humanity headlong into a relationship marred by sin and shame. How could creation possibly hope to be restored to the Creator? It seemed there was no path to lead them and us back.

But now through Jesus Christ and the amazing grace of God, we are drawn back to that love relationship and that place of purity and perfect fellowship with Him.

For those who overcome and truly fall head over heels in love with the Savior and never stop pursuing His heart, they are given the right to reach out and take hold of the Tree of Life—the eternal, immortal life, which is the inheritance of those who love Him. What Adam and Eve could no longer grab hold of is now within our reach because of Jesus.

Concerning the one who overcomes, repents, and returns to this first love, Albert Barnes says in his commentary,

> He is thus restored to what he might have been if he had not transgressed by eating of the fruit of the tree of the knowledge of good and evil; and in the Paradise Regained, the blessings of the Paradise Lost will be more than recovered-for man may now live forever in a far higher and more blessed state than his would have been in Eden. (Barnes, 1834).

When we return to our first love and are restored in a right relationship, what was taken away from us when sin entered in will be restored, and we will have the blessing to eat of the Tree of Life in heaven. We will live forever with the one who first loved us!

We will have eternal life in the presence of Jehovah! What an incredible promise for those who overcome!

I want this to get into your heart and mind. Whatever it seems the Enemy has stolen from you, whatever appears to have been taken away and forever lost, whatever you have surrendered and now desire to regain can be restored fully and abundantly.

First Samuel 30 records a story that gives some insight into this principle. The scene of this story opens with David and his men returning to their city in Ziklag. They had left the city *unguarded* to go and ally themselves with the Philistines to do battle.

That was their first mistake, and it is ours as well. If we leave ourselves unguarded, we are asking for trouble. This is why Scripture admonishes us to "guard our hearts and minds in Christ Jesus" (Philippians 4:6-8 NKJV).

Being rejected by the Philistines, David and his men returned to their home camp and found the Amalekites had invaded Ziklag and burned it to the ground. The enemies of David had taken captive all the wives and children of these men and stolen all their goods.

Suddenly David's own men turned against him and wanted to stone him. He found himself in a place of complete and utter loss! His family was gone. His possessions were gone, and now the devotion and loyalty of his men was being stripped away!

The Scripture tells us David and the men surrounding him "wept until they could weep no more." The sixth verse says that David strengthened himself in the Lord, his God, and he inquired of the Lord as to what he should do!

When he had no strength, no tears, and no hope left within himself, David found his resolve in his first love of God! He was brought back to the place of surrender and intimacy with God that he had cultivated when he was just a boy tending his father's sheep.

He sought the Lord, and through his relationship with God, he was strengthened and advised on what he needed to do to turn the situation around! He asked God, "Shall I pursue this troop? Shall I overtake them?"

God answered him and said, "Pursue, for you shall surely overtake them and without fail recover all!" That is just what David did! Every wife, every child, every possession was unharmed and returned and not only that. David soundly defeated the enemy and took the spoils of the Amalekites!

It doesn't matter what it seems the enemy has stolen in your life. God says fall in love with Him, be strengthened in your spirit, rise up from the place of defeat and complacency, and go forward in the process of victory and restoration!

You might be reading this right now after your marriage or family has fallen apart and the Enemy seems to have left you in pieces on the ground. Perhaps you have experienced a loss, financial loss, death of a loved one, end of a relationship, or loss of health. The first thing you need to do is *run* to God!

In your love relationship with Him, you will be dressed in the garments of an overcomer. You can see those losses and devastations turned around, and God can give back to you more than the Enemy has stolen!

John Wycliffe said, "First love is the love of espousal. Its notes are simplicity, and purity, marital love, the response of love to love, the subjection of a great love to a great love, the submission of a self-denying love to a love that denies self. First love is the abandonment of all for a love that has abandoned all." (Wycliffe, 1384)

When we come back to our first love, there is beauty, simplicity, and purity again in our love for the Lord. All the things we *do* for Him will then be an extension of our true love *for* Him. When we come back to Him, we will find ourselves lost *in* His love rather than lost *from* His love!

Love is the first place we must begin!

~

If I speak in the tongues of men or of angels, but do not have love, I am only a resounding gong or a clanging cymbal. If I have the gift

of prophecy and can fathom all mysteries and all knowledge, and
if I have a faith that can move mountains, but do not have love, I
am nothing. If I give all I possess to the poor and give over my body
to hardship that I may boast, but do not have love, I gain nothing.
Love is patient, love is kind. It does not envy, it does not boast, it is
not proud. It does not dishonor others, it is not self-seeking, it is not
easily angered, it keeps no record of wrongs. Love does not delight
in evil but rejoices with the truth. It always protects, always trusts,
always hopes, always perseveres. Love never fails. And now these
three remain: faith, hope and love. But the greatest of these is love.

—1 Corinthians 13: 1–8, 13 (NKJV)

CHAPTER 3

Faithfulness Has Its Rewards! Church of Smryna

And to the angel of the church in Smyrna write,
"These things says the First and the Last, who was dead, and
came to life: 'I know your works, tribulation, and poverty (but
you are rich); and I know the blasphemy of those who say they
are Jews and are not, but are a synagogue of Satan. Do not fear
any of those things which you are about to suffer. Indeed, the
devil is about to throw some of you into prison, that you may
be tested, and you will have tribulation ten days. Be faithful
until death, and I will give you the crown of life. He who has
an ear, let him hear what the Spirit says to the churches. He
who overcomes shall not be hurt by the second death.'"

—Revelation 2:8–11 (NKJV)

The church of Smyrna was a body of believers who found themselves
in a position where what they held dear, their faith in Christ, was
bringing them to a time of severe persecution and suffering as they

had never before known. The source of this letter is from the one who is the first and the last, who was dead and is now alive, which clearly refers to Jesus Christ.

It is worth noting that Christ never condemns this church in any way but speaks of the things their faithfulness is and will bring upon them. What is even more interesting is the contrast between the economy of this world and the economy of the kingdom of God!

There is an erroneous mind-set that says if we don't have a lot of money in the bank, then we are not being blessed by God or we must be doing something wrong or God doesn't love us. Too frequently we judge the prosperity of a person's faith and salvation on the way the world looks at prosperity. If certain people have enough money and few trials, we think that God is blessing them and that they must be spiritual giants. On the flip side of this, if certain people find themselves lacking or dealing with health issues or big problems in their lives, we wonder how small their faith is and what they did wrong to deserve that punishment.

God's economy and God's view of prosperity has nothing to do with the size of our bank accounts, our assets, or how well things seem to be going in our lives. Man looks on the outward appearance and judges success or failure by the view they have with their natural eye. However, God looks far beyond all the fluff and superficiality of material things and good situations because these things often give a deceptive view of the true reality.

God sees the heart, the mind, the intent, the spirit, and the faith of a person and judges the person's life by who he or she really is and not by what that individual has or what is going on in his or her life. It must be established in our hearts that the economy (success, finances, wealth, or poverty) of this world is vastly different than God's economy. Such is the case of the church in Smyrna.

This group of believers appears to be a poor church in a wealthy city! There is no indication why the church was poor, but perhaps it was because of the hatred and persecution of Christianity, which seemed to be growing in many regions. This church seems to have been filled with men and women who were strong in their faith and faithful to the gospel and yet were experiencing economic poverty.

The Lord spoke to this church and said even though on the outside it appears you have nothing, you are rich! How incredible would it be to hear the Lord speak that blessing over you?

I know it looks as if you are destitute. I know you can't see what tomorrow holds. I know you don't understand how all your bills are going to be paid. I know you don't know where your next paycheck is coming from. However, I see the size of the faith that thrives in you, and I want you to know *you are rich!*

I want the Lord to look at my life and see beyond what I don't have in the natural and see what I do have in the spiritual! Our prayer should be this: "Father, look beyond all my failures, misgivings, and lack and see my heart!"

It is out of the richness of their spiritual lives they would be able to see the hand of God even through the things they would face. During times of persecution, hatred, and difficulty, money would not help them at all, but a strong abiding faith in Jesus Christ would see them through to victory.

Look for the handiwork of God in everything you go through because He is ordering your steps. Even though life may take you through moments of distress and persecution, still God is there working all things together for your benefit and your good.

In the middle of the trial it may not look like anything positive can come out of it, but rest assured He is weaving the tapestry of your life as He leads you step by step and moment by moment. Eventually you will see the full picture and be amazed at the providence and creativity of God.

Every Christian and every church will go through times of testing and trial. In this testing there is a strengthening and a purification of the body of Christ.

One of the blessings of severe persecution is that the church always seems to come together stronger than it ever has before. We tend to lay aside petty differences and divisions for the sake of the body. We forget about previous hurts and offenses to rally together in the face of the attacks of the Enemy.

When we intentionally disregard the things that separate us, it brings a powerful unity to the body of Christ, and this is no more visible than when the church undergoes some type of persecution.

The same similarity can be seen in a family that is close-knit. It is all right for the family members to fuss and argue and disagree with one another all day long; however, let an outsider say something against one of their family members, and they join forces together as a family unit to protect and guard that family member.

Outside persecution brings inside unity!

The Lord began to unfold to the church of Smyrna the plan of the Devil and those adversaries who were trying to destroy the gospel in that city. This probably wasn't easy for these people to hear. Perhaps they were hoping for a word that was positive and uplifting because they had already been through so much and had held on tightly to their faith. Nevertheless, the word came out as a warning of the plans of those who were against them!

However, it is interesting to note that the Lord began by telling them not to fear!

Fear is a tool the Enemy has been using against God's people for far too long. Fear has kept so many good people from standing up in their anointing. Fear has paralyzed millions from taking the next step of faith. Fear has shut the mouths of multitudes from proclaiming what they should have proclaimed. Fear has emasculated the warriors of the army of the Lord. Fear has held the children of God as prisoners of war. Fear has weakened and incapacitated. Fear has divided and destroyed.

But God has not given us a spirit of fear (2 Timothy 1:7). We need to declare that over ourselves right now! Go ahead and proclaim that over your life right now! *God has not given me a spirit of fear!*

He has given us a spirit of power, love, and self-discipline! There is a building process going on here. When we come back to our first love in Jesus Christ, we begin to walk in an understanding of the Scripture in 1 John 4:18, which says, "There is no fear in *love;* but *perfect love* casts out fear." Because we love God and He loves us, we don't have to live in fear but can know the perfect love and courage of the Lord Jesus Christ.

Fear comes from our Enemy, but we do not have to fear him. Satan may wage war. He may rant and rave. He can try to intimidate and terrify you; however, we know to whom we belong, and He is the first and the last! He is the first... the one who created everything, and He is the last. He is the final judge and will have the final word! You must remember that greater is He that lives within you than the bully who comes against you!

The church in Smyrna was told that many of them would be persecuted, thrown into prison, and have their faith tested. Hypocrites and blasphemers would falsely condemn them and cause them to be imprisoned or killed. This was the plan of the Devil against them. The battle plan had been carefully and strategically organized by their Enemy and would soon be executed. Just as God had a plan for them to go forward with the message of the gospel in that city, the Enemy also had a plan to stop them and silence their message!

Are you aware that the Enemy of your soul has a plan to destroy what God wants to do in you?

Did you know that he levels his attacks at you because he knows God's hand and anointing is upon you?

Do you also understand that, just as the Lord did in this passage of Scripture, God can expose the plans of the Enemy and give you strength to face the invasion?

God may not always stop the hand of the Enemy from performing his plan, but God can give you the power to be an overcomer through it all!

This is my favorite part of this letter because it assures me that God knows my life and path and that He also knows the Enemy and what he is planning to do to me. God shows up, tells on the Devil, and exposes all his plans! *I love it!*

God knows all the Devil's intel. He has bugged the Devil's command center! Your life is so important to God that when He needs to, He will reveal to you what Satan is planning and what you need to do to overcome him. This is one of the reasons we must continually walk in a close, sensitive relationship to Jesus Christ. This is why He must be our first love!

Faithfulness to the things of God will give us access to privileged information. Armed with that information, we can continue to faithfully follow the spirit of God and destroy the works of the Enemy!

I know this because the next words of the prophecy to Smyrna say, "Be faithful until death and I will give you the crown of life" (Revelation 2:10b NKJV). The Lord encourages them to look beyond the persecution to the greater good and be faithful just like He did when He endured the cross of Calvary, fixing His eyes on the prize, fulfilling the Father's plan, namely salvation for you and me. The love Jesus has for humanity caused Him to look beyond the pain, the weakness, the suffering, and the rejection of Calvary and see redemption for each one of us. Thank You, Lord!

He wasn't promising them everything was going to be easy. He never insinuated there wouldn't be difficulties. He didn't even promise that all of them would come out alive here on the earth. God simply said to the church of Smyrna, "Be faithful!"

If there is anything the Holy Spirit is saying to the church today in this postmodern society, perhaps it is just that: "Be faithful!" There is a reward at the end. A crown of life awaits you. When He comes, He will be looking for faith, and He will find it in the faithful. Just as He has been faithful to us, we must strive to be faithful to Him!

When Paul and Silas were sitting in the Philippian prison after they had been beaten and chained, they still were not defeated! The whole reason they found themselves in this predicament was because they were doing the work of the kingdom.

Nevertheless, things were about to change because around the midnight hour faith began to rise up within them. Their bodies were bloody. Their freedom was gone. They were shackled in a prison, and yet their faith was still fully intact.

What the Enemy doesn't seem to understand is that he can't imprison the faith of the faithful. You can beat them, mistreat them, cheat them, lie about them, gossip about them, and throw their bodies in a smelly old jail, but the faith that lies within them will emerge and change everything.

Paul and Silas didn't focus on their persecution or the accusations or their present accommodations. They set their sights on the author and the finisher (first and last) of their faith, and they began to pray and sing and have a Holy Ghost revival right there in the prison!

There is something amazing here I want to make sure you see. Because of the faithfulness and praise of Paul and Silas, *every single prisoner* in the jail was set free from their shackles and chains! That's pretty powerful!

When we are faithful in good times and bad, when we praise him during the day and the darkest night, it will not only set us free, but it will begin to set others around us free as well!

If you want freedom in your life, then begin to praise Him through the trial. You want freedom in your family, then lift your hands and begin to worship in the middle of the fight. It is liberating!

You shake up the Enemy when he is trying to attack you and rather than running in fear, your hands are raised and you are praising God! When you do that, God inhabits your praise, and where His Spirit and presence are, there is freedom!

In Revelation 2:11, the Scripture gives this promise to the overcomer: "He who has an ear let him hear what the Spirit says to the churches. He who overcomes shall not be hurt by the second death."

"Death cuts off from life—and so the second death cuts off from eternal life; death puts an end to all our hopes here, and the second death to all our hopes forever" (Barnes's notes, 1834).

In this world we will experience tribulation and persecution. God warned us that there would be times when all we can do is hold on to the faith that is deep inside us. Times of persecution will more often than not be indicative of just how firm and deep our faith is in the Lord. If we overcome these problematic seasons in our lives, we have been promised that the second death will have no effect on us.

This second death of which John speaks is the eternal death and separation from God, which the unrighteous will experience in eternity. The Bible says, "It is appointed unto man once to die" (Hebrews 9:27). This speaks of a physical, earthly death.

The second death though is dying an eternal death. This separation from the presence of God is permanent and eternal. Once the second death has taken its toll, the results are irreversible.

When loved ones die on this earth, we dress them up, make them up, do their hair, place them in a casket, and lay them to rest, or if it is their wishes, we will have them cremated and scatter their ashes to their place of rest. In this second death of which John wrote, there is no rest.

It is written in the Word of God that this second death is not a place of rest but of fire, torment, wailing, gnashing of teeth, and isolation from the presence of their Creator. Those who overcome in this life will escape the second death and will find eternal joy, peace, and rest in the presence of Jehovah!

Because Jesus is the only one who was dead and is now alive (Revelation 2:8), He is the only one who has the right to make this promise. The Son of God is the only one death could not conquer. He is the one that death could not hold down, the one who rose victorious over death, hell, and the grave. So He alone is the one who can stop the power of the second death over those who have been faithful and who have overcome!

I know life can show no mercy at times. Situations can pound on our soul, mind, and body like the wind and rain pound on a house during a hurricane. I understand when we have been persecuted, wrongly judged, lied about, treated unfairly, and misunderstood, the desire to just give up can become very overwhelming. However, we must hold on!

There may be some who will go to prison for the gospel, some who may be beaten or tortured, some who may be rejected and despised, some who may lay down their lives for Jesus Christ, but through it all we must remain strong. This is of utmost importance in the heart of a believer. There is a prize at the end of this race! The crown of life awaits! Faithfulness does have rewards!

No matter what life throws at you, remember that, according to the Word of God, you are a joint heir with Jesus Christ. Romans 8:16–18 (NKJV) says,

> The Spirit Himself bears witness with our spirit that we are children of God, and if children, then heirs—heirs of God and joint heirs with Christ, if indeed we suffer with Him, that we may also be glorified together. For I consider that the sufferings of this present time are not worthy to be compared with the glory which shall be revealed in us.

The struggles we deal with on this earth cannot even begin to compare with what we will receive in heaven if we overcome! The difficulties today that seem so insurmountable and impossible will seem small and trivial when we see Jesus in all His glory. There is a reward! So don't give up.

Whether your life's journey takes you to the top of the mountain or to the depths of the valley, you can make it! When you have come through on the other side of the trial, God's glory will be revealed in you, and you will stand as a trophy of His grace! Keep your eyes on the prize.

~

Therefore we also, since we are surrounded by so great a cloud of witnesses, let us lay aside every weight, and the sin which so easily ensnares us, and let us run with endurance the race that is set before us, looking unto Jesus, the author and finisher of our faith, who for the joy that was set before Him endured the cross, despising the shame, and has sat down at the right hand of the throne of God. For consider Him who endured such hostility from sinners against Himself, lest you become weary and discouraged in your souls.

—Hebrews 12:1–3 (NKJV)

CHAPTER 4

Repentance... Not a Suggestion... A Requirement! Church of Pergamos

And to the angel of the church in Pergamos write, "These things says He who has the sharp two-edged sword: 'I know your works, and where you dwell, where Satan's throne is. And you hold fast to My name, and did not deny My faith even in the days in which Antipas was My faithful martyr, who was killed among you, where Satan dwells. But I have a few things against you, because you have there those who hold the doctrine of Balaam, who taught Balak to put a stumbling block before the children of Israel, to eat things sacrificed to idols, and to commit sexual immorality. Thus you also have those who hold the doctrine of the Nicolaitans, which thing I hate. Repent, or else I will come to you quickly and will fight against them with the sword of My mouth. He who has an ear, let him hear what the Spirit says to the churches. To him who overcomes I will give some of the hidden manna to eat. And I will give him a white stone, and on the stone a new name written which no one knows except him who receives it.'"

—Revelation 2:12–17 (NKJV)

This letter to Pergamos comes straight from the one who has the sharp two-edged sword. Who is this person? It is easy to deduce that the author of this letter is none other than Jesus Christ Himself. In the first chapter of Revelation while John is unfolding the vision given to him, he describes the glorious manifestation of Jesus by saying,

> Then I turned to see the voice that spoke with me. And having turned I saw seven golden lampstands, and in the midst of the seven lampstands One like the Son of Man, clothed with a garment down to the feet and girded about the chest with a golden band. His head and hair were white like wool, as white as snow, and His eyes like a flame of fire; His feet were like fine brass, as if refined in a furnace, and His voice as the sound of many waters; He had in His right hand seven stars, out of His mouth went a sharp two-edged sword, and His countenance was like the sun shining in its strength. (Revelation 1:12–16)

This same Jesus whom John saw spoke with power and authority to the church at Pergamos. There is something about a two-edged sword that is more intimidating and strikes more fear in the heart than a regular sword or weapon. A two-edged sword has the power to cut and divide whether it is being plunged in or withdrawn. Because of the sharpness of both sides of the sword, it has the potential to pierce deeper and cut more profoundly.

Hebrews 4:12 (NKJV) shows the similarity between the Word of God and a two-edged sword. This passage reads, "For the word of God is living and powerful, and sharper than any two-edged sword, piercing even to the division of soul and spirit, and of joints and marrow, and is a discerner of the thoughts and intents of the heart."

The joints and marrow of the human body are correlated with the soul and spirit of humanity. Just as a two-edged sword can pierce the body and affect the joints and marrow, which lie hidden within the bones and body of a person, so the Word of God can penetrate to the hidden and deep places of the soul and spirit. Nothing else can reach those places we hide from others. Nothing but the Word of God can cut through the layers of rubbish we pile on our lives to try to disguise our heart!

So the importance here is that the church at Pergamos must (and likewise we must) hear, understand, and fear the words that come from the mouth of God, who has the two-edged sword. His words can either cut things away and bring life and health or cut things through and bring judgment and death.

It is an intimidating thing to know that He is the discerner of our thoughts, the intentions of our actions, and the meditations of our minds. We can hide a lot of things from our families, friends, and fellow church members, but the Word of God will cut away everything and expose that which we try to hide. It's a matter of pruning or prosecution, blessing or cursing, mercy or judgment, life or death.

Just as He has spoken to the other churches, He tells the church at Pergamos, "I know your works." He began by commending them for the things they had done. He not only knew their deeds, but he knew the place they lived and the extenuating circumstances with which they had to deal. Pergamos must have been a place of unprecedented evil because it is referred to as the place where the throne of Satan exists. It was a city steeped in mysticism and occult practices.

Many times living for the Lord can be difficult simply because of where we live. There are regions and areas of this world that are known to be places where there is an overwhelming amount of spiritual wickedness and evil, nations or cities where occult or cultic activities saturate the area. There are other places where promiscuity and perversion are not only present but welcomed. There are cities, counties, and countries where the Enemy has set up certain strongholds and high places for spiritual wickedness.

Pergamos had become a hub for false religions and pagan cults, and perhaps this is why it was referred to as the place "where Satan's throne is." There was a lot of idolatry and demonic activity associated with this city, and it had become a difficult place to follow Christ and live righteously. The members of the church in this city found themselves constantly dealing with the presence of evil, and spiritual warfare was not only a daily occurrence but something they fought every minute.

There are certain places and circumstances where it is easier to live for God, situations where there is comfort and we don't have to be involved in spiritual warfare, places where there is no persecution and life is not hard, cities where revival is happening and you can sense an overwhelming presence of the Holy Spirit. In these places it is often easier to "take up your cross and follow Him."

It's simple to live right and be holy in the middle of an amazing worship service or altar call. We can more easily do what is right when we are surrounded by godly influences and people who are living holy lives.

But what about those places where it seems we are constantly bombarded on every side by an attack of the Enemy. Perhaps you are in a city that is saturated with demonic or occult activity. It could be you live in a place where your eyes, ears, and mind are constantly assaulted with sexual or perverted images. What about those places where there are no mountains and all we seem to experience is valley?

Living victoriously in those places can be extremely trying and difficult. There may be times when you are so influenced by these things you feel like you can't go on. You tell yourself, "It's just useless. I can't do it! I can't fight this battle one more time! I can't face this temptation again. I can't deal with this sin or this hurt or this rejection anymore!" But listen to me closely. No matter where you find yourself geographically, spiritually, emotionally, or mentally, you are *more* than a conqueror through Jesus Christ, who loves you and gave Himself for you!

No matter how fierce the battle, there is victory in the name of Jesus and by the power of the Holy Spirit. If you wait upon the Lord, you can mount up on wings like an eagle! Don't let the place or the situation or the battle dictate your walk with God because He knows your works. When it feels like all your strength is gone because of the struggle, let God's strength arise in you.

Second Corinthians 12:9–10 (NKJV) tells us, "My grace is sufficient for you, for My strength is made perfect in weakness. Therefore most gladly I will rather boast in my infirmities, that the power of Christ may rest upon me. Therefore I take pleasure in infirmities, in reproaches, in needs, in persecutions, in distresses, for Christ's sake. For when I am weak, then I am strong."

In order to determine the true strength of an overcomer, we first have to know what this person has walked through in his or her life that has brought the individual to the place he or she is today! Each one of us has our own testimony and our own story of what God has brought us through. Some have been blessed to deal with little persecutions or tragedies in their lives while others seem to have walked through the very pit of hell itself.

Who are we to look down in condemnation on people who are still fighting the fight and struggling? Maybe their walks of faith have taken them to places ours has not taken us. It could be that if we had to live through what they have had to live through, our faith might have taken a plunge long before now!

There is an account in the Bible in Luke 8:43–48 about a woman who pressed through and received what she needed from the Lord. This lady had suffered with health issues for twelve long years. She had spent all of her money on doctors to try to get well, and yet she found herself hopelessly confined to this sickness. Day after day she carried on, hoping beyond hope that this would be the day she would finally get some relief.

One day as Jesus was on His way somewhere else with someone else to minister to someone else, this little woman decided, "This could be my last chance. I know He is not in town to see me and He doesn't even know I'm here, but this is my moment for breakthrough. If I don't get this now, I will die!"

She didn't let the place, the circumstances, or the insurmountable nature of the situation detour or stop her. She pressed in through the crowd that was surrounding Jesus. No one else knew why she was there. Everyone else was clueless about her predicament. Possibly no one else knew what she had been through and why she was so adamant about pushing her way through the crowd. The people in the crowd paid her no attention and didn't care about her emergency.

I can just see her as she looks for and can't find an opening through the throng of people. She gets down on her hands and knees and begins to crawl her way past people's dirty, smelly feet and sweaty legs just to get close enough to touch Jesus. I can also imagine that when she, as a last desperate attempt, reached that little hand out, full of faith, and she made contact with just the hem of His garment, victory and healing flooded into her life. The very cure she had longed for and hoped for now became a reality! Everything changed for her in that moment because she didn't let her situation or her physical weakness steal the miracle and healing God had destined for her.

Notice this: Just as with the church in Pergamos, Jesus knew her works because he stopped the crowd and asked His disciples who had touched Him. His disciples assured Him there were so many people around Him that lots of people had likely touched Him, but He knew! He knew someone had reached out in faith. He was fully sensitive to every elbow, shoulder, and hand that touched Him. He recognized the difference between someone in the crowd just pushing against Him and someone touching Him with a touch of faith that would change a life.

The faith of someone in distress had attached itself to His power, and it flowed out of Him. The woman confessed, and Jesus told her that she was made whole because of her faith!

Just as she had held on to her faith, this was the commendation of the church in Pergamos that they held onto the name of Jesus and did not deny His faith even after they saw the martyrdom of one of the men of the city who had been faithful to the gospel.

Yet still the Lord had a few things against them!

Commentator Brian Pepper says, "The church which had suffered so much for the sake of the Gospel has allowed certain corruptions to enter the church and spoil its purity."

The church had compromised and allowed the doctrines of Balaam and the Nicolatians to be tolerated in their church. These were doctrines of greed, idolatry, sexual immorality, and a belief that the grace of Christ completely did away with the law of God, so they could profess the name of Christ and pursue their sinful lusts and claim they were still saved. This belief system is erroneous and dangerous. These were things that Christ hated, and yet if we are not careful, these same beliefs can find their way into our lives and our churches today.

Remember, according to 2 Corinthians 5:10 (NKJV), "We must all appear before the judgment seat of Christ." It would be foolish not to ask God to search us and know us and see if there is a hurtful way in us (Psalm 139).

We live in a society that finds its treasure in tolerance and acceptance of anything that calls itself religion or a belief. We have become a melting pot of religious activity, and yet the relationship with Christ that leads us to holiness and purity is being compromised for the sake of sensitivity and political correctness.

The church finds herself with mounting pressure to conform to the belief systems of the world, and if the church does, then she opens her doors to all kinds of perverseness, unbiblical agendas and errant theologies.

Unbeknownst to him, when Lot chose to leave Abraham and head toward the land that looked green and fruitful, he was headed for disaster. As he settled in the city of Sodom, this place of wickedness eventually began to take a toll on his faith and his family! The sins and practices of this community were detestable enough within themselves, but the judgment of God came because of their unwillingness to repent. Their hearts had become so deceived and set on what they found pleasure in that even though God sent His angel, they would not forsake their desires and passions to seek God. Living in this environment day after day will have an impact on individuals and can easily turn their hearts and minds away from what is true and right!

The degree of this entrenchment of wickedness in Sodom and Gomorrah is shocking. God sent His angels to Sodom to rescue Lot and his family, and the men of the city became so overcome with lust that they demanded Lot send the angels out to them so they could rape them and satisfy their own passions.

Understand this: The people in Sodom didn't start out this way, but through the years one compromise led to another. As time went by, one justification of their actions piled on top of a second and then a third and a fourth until the day arrived when the men of this city were morally depraved and could not even recognize the error of their thoughts and actions.

This was a serious issue in the church of Pergamos because many true believers were being led away from Christ and into beliefs that they could live in immorality and sin and still be right! But this mind-set is an abomination to the one who has the two-edged sword. Although the whole church was not adhering to these false beliefs, the problem arose because they were allowing them to be there and tolerating them.

The church and individual Christians must do everything we can to guard ourselves and the body of Christ against false teaching and heresy. If we do not protect our hearts and minds, the truth will quickly be removed from us, and lies mixed with enough truth to sound right will become what we consume and believe.

Jesus told the church that if they did not repent immediately, then He would come quickly and fight against them with the sword of His mouth. This sword represents judgment. This message wasn't for the heathen. This was spoken to the church!

God didn't do like many of us do with our children today. He didn't say, "I'm going to count to three, and if you don't repent, then there will be consequences." He didn't offer them the option of being put in a time-out until they came to their senses and repented. No! He spoke plainly concerning the way it would be if they did not turn from this wickedness and then said His punishment would be swift and severe.

I know judgment is not a pretty word. In this day and age people don't want a God who judges them. A Creator who evaluates the hearts of mankind is not desirable to a person who wants to live as he or she pleases without repercussions. These people want to be able to act and speak however they see fit and not have to answer to anyone for it. However, when we begin to allow things to remain in our lives that shouldn't be there, it will bring the judgment of God.

Little things that seem as if they don't really matter *do matter*! King Solomon is quoted as saying, "It is the little foxes that spoil the vine" (Song of Solomon 2:15 NKJV). The small, seemingly insignificant compromises we allow will eventually spoil and steal our victory. The choices we make and the things we believe make a big difference in our lives as an overcomer. They will decide if we walk in victory or defeat, acquittal or judgment!

The judgment is the words of God's mouth, which are powerful and effective to accomplish His purpose. The same God who created everything that exists by the words He spoke can also execute judgment simply by speaking it into being!

The thoughts, attitudes, or actions we permit to remain in our lives or in our churches, even when we know they are wrong, will bring with them consequences. Many times there are severe consequences unless we repent. As you can see, there is a way to elude judgment. We don't have to face the wrath or discipline of God.

True repentance will bring a change of heart and actions. True repentance will deal with and deliver us from the issues in our lives that have brought us to the place of impending judgment. The scary thing is that we have generally become so comfortable with the things in our lives that displease God that we no longer see them as problems. We also see no reason to change them. We make justifications rather than adjustments for the sin in our lives. This only leads us further away from victory!

The Holy Spirit can bring illumination to our hearts if we ask Him to come in and clean house. He will reveal the things we need to remove from our lives in order to experience the favor and blessing of God rather than His judgment! True victory is when, in complete obedience to the will of God, we clean house at His prompting. No excuses, no reasoning, no arguing, just simple and complete obedience in repentance.

Look at the story recorded in John 2:13–16 (NKJV),

> Now the Passover of the Jews was at hand, and Jesus went up to Jerusalem. And He found in the temple those who sold oxen and sheep and doves, and the money changers doing business. When He had made a whip of cords, He drove them all out of the temple, with the sheep and the oxen, and poured out the changers' money and overturned the tables. And He said to those who sold doves, "Take these things away! Do not make My Father's house a house of merchandise!"

This event gives us insight and discernment into how we should deal with sin, false beliefs, errant doctrines, fear, and all that displeases God. These should be dealt with quickly and brutally. God never winks at sin. God doesn't shrug His shoulders at those things that would corrupt His creation. Our Holy God won't just smile and remain quiet about the things that would keep us from fulfilling the purpose and destiny for which He has created us.

The temple was the place where the presence of God dwelt. It was supposed to represent all that was holy and righteous. The temple represented their link to the throne of God. This is why God gave such specific details to the builders of the temple. He had a divine purpose for it! Yet there were those who would come in and defile the temple by turning it into a marketplace rather than the house of prayer and worship, which is what it was designed to be. So what does that have to do with me? How does that affect my life here in the twenty-first century?

Compromise offered to that which is contrary to God's Word is never something that should be part of a believer's life. Once you jeopardize the purity of your walk with Christ by allowing wrong thoughts, attitudes, actions, or beliefs, you open a gateway for other problems to arise.

I preached a sermon once titled "Compromise and Cockroaches." Compromise is kind of like when you find a roach in your home. If you immediately kill it and spray to take care of the problem, then chances are that you won't find any others (and if you do, they will be dead). But if you find one and do not take quick action to rid your home of it, then before you know it, that one has another friend, and they tell another friend and so on and so on. Before you even realize it, you have a roach infestation, and you have to call in the professionals to exterminate them because it has quickly become a much bigger problem than you can handle.

So it is with sin in our lives. We must hold fast to that which we believe and not give in, compromise, or allow the smallest hint of negotiation! Few reach the place of true conquest and victory because they consistently compromise in the small things and it eats away and erodes the foundation of their relationship with God like waves can erode the seashore.

Those small compromises quickly multiply until there is an unmanageable infestation. How can we overcome if we are allowing the "little roaches of the Enemy" to steal our attention and victory?

Psalm 119:2–4 (NLT) encourages us in this way: "Joyful are those who obey his laws and search for him with all their hearts. They do not compromise with evil, and they walk only in his paths. You have charged us to keep your commandments carefully."

It is our responsibility and privilege to uphold the standard of absolute truth, righteousness, and holiness given to us by God in His Word. We can never compromise with evil or bargain with sin. Just as the United States of America has a policy that we will not negotiate with terrorists, so we must institute this policy in our lives when it comes to the Terrorist of our soul.

Revelation 2:17 (NKJV) states, "He who has an ear, let him hear what the Spirit says to the churches. To him who overcomes I will give some of the hidden manna to eat. And I will give him a white stone, and on the stone a new name written which no one knows except him who receives it."

Speaking of this hidden manna Albert Barnes wrote,

> The Hebrews were supported by manna in the desert (Exodus 16:16–35), and a pot of that manna was laid up in the most holy place to be preserved as a memorial (Exodus 16:32–34). It is called angel's food (Psalm 78:25) and bread of heaven (Psalm 78:24), and it would seem to have been emblematic of that spiritual food by which the people of God are to be fed from heaven in their journey through this world (Barnes, 1834).

This is an indication that when we overcome and He lives in the temple of our lives, we will be continuously nourished by the bread of His presence. It is a delicacy that not everyone in this world is able to taste, only those who overcome. We see that true victory is so sweet. When we are feasting on the buffet of victory, we don't think about the fierceness of the battle. This manna will provide our sustenance in this earthly life and in our eternal life as well! It is the bread of heaven.

When the nation of Israel was fed and nourished by manna in the wilderness, God gave them exactly what they needed for that day—nothing more and nothing less. Their provision was to get them through the present circumstances! God will provide for us exactly what we need at exactly the moment we need it in order to strengthen us and give us success in our journey to victorious lives.

He has promised also that we will receive a white stone with a new name on it. In biblical times the judges and court systems would announce their verdicts by giving the accused either a white stone or a black stone. The white stone represented that the individual had been acquitted of the crime, and the person could go free. The black stone showed the person was guilty of the crime and deserved the punishment he or she would receive.

If you stood in the courtroom of God today, would there be fear and concern in your heart about your guilt or innocence? Are there things in your life that would render a guilty verdict and produce a black stone?

Revelation 12:10 tells us that there is an accuser of the people of God and that he accuses them before God day and night. There is an accuser out there right now who is pointing a finger at you and telling God that you are *guilty!* Satan is announcing to God that you deserve the punishment of your sin/crime, which is death.

This accuser is replaying all your past transgressions before the Lord. As the prosecutor, he is doing his best to prove that you are sinful. Yet when God as the judge looks at your life and He sees the blood of Jesus and the spirit of an overcomer in you, He won't condemn you. When He sees your sights set on victory, He will fight for you! When He sees you worshipping in a pure and clean temple, strong and nourished with the manna from heaven, He will arise and hand you a white stone and say, "You are set free!" Freedom is yours today! Let me say that again because someone needs to know this: *Freedom is yours today!*

On this white stone is a new name. The Israelites would be familiar with this idea of a stone with a name on it because when the high priest would put on his priestly garments, one of those items would be a breastplate, and on that breastplate were twelve stones. Each one was inscribed with the name of one of the twelve tribes of Israel (those who belonged to the house and family of God). Those names represented inclusion in the kingdom of God.

It is not known what this new name is, but perhaps this new name written on the white stone is a name of adoption and inheritance, which He will give those who overcome. It could be that this is your new name in the family and house of God because you have held on and not given in. There is an eternal inheritance that goes along with this acquittal. Those who overcome will forever be in the temple of God, feasting on that heavenly manna, which is the fullness of His presence and glory. They will never hunger or thirst again. There will be no more conflicts or struggles.

~

> You prepare a table before me in the presence of my enemies; You anoint my head with oil; My cup runs over. Surely goodness and mercy shall follow me all the days of my life; And I will dwell in the house of the Lord forever.

—Psalm 23:5–6 (NKJV)

CHAPTER 5

Run Strong and Avoid Detours! Church of Thyatira

And to the angel of the church in Thyatira write, "These things says the Son of God, who has eyes like a flame of fire, and His feet like fine brass: 'I know your works, love, service, faith, and your patience; and as for your works, the last are more than the first. Nevertheless I have a few things against you, because you allow that woman Jezebel, who calls herself a prophetess, to teach and seduce My servants to commit sexual immorality and eat things sacrificed to idols. And I gave her time to repent of her sexual immorality, and she did not repent. Indeed I will cast her into a sickbed, and those who commit adultery with her into great tribulation, unless they repent of their deeds. I will kill her children with death, and all the churches shall know that I am He who searches the minds and hearts. And I will give to each one of you according to your works. Now to you I say, and to the rest in Thyatira, as many as do not have this doctrine, who have not known the depths of Satan, as they say, I will put on you no other burden. But hold fast what you have till I come. And he who overcomes, and keeps My works until the end, to him I will give power over the nations. He shall rule them with a rod of iron; They shall be dashed to pieces like the potter's vessels as I also have received from My Father; and I will give him the morning star. He who has an ear, let him hear what the Spirit says to the churches.'"

—Revelation 2:18–29 (NKJV)

This letter also was from the Son of God, Jesus Christ. It was written to the church in Thyatira for their encouragement and also for their rebuke. Concerning the appearance of the Son of God in this instance, commentator Matthew Henry writes,

> That His eyes are like a flame of fire, signifying His piercing, penetrating, perfect knowledge, a thorough insight into all persons and all things, One who searches the hearts and tries the reins of the children of men, and will make all the churches to know He does so. That His feet are like fine brass, that the outgoings of His providence are steady, awful, and all pure and holy. As He judges with perfect wisdom, so He acts with perfect strength and steadiness.

In this perfect knowledge and strength, Christ knew the works of this church. How remarkable is His compliment of their love, service, patience, and faith. Their works were so incredible that Jesus said the last ones were better than the first ones. This means they had not become weary in well doing. They had not gotten casual or careless about the work they were doing. The ministries they were accomplishing now were even better than they were when they had first begun. There was a continual perfecting and excellence in what they were achieving. They were being fruitful in greater ways, and the fruits of their ministries were evident.

Generally we have a tendency to start strong and finish tired and weak, if we finish at all! We commit ourselves to the Lord or a ministry or a relationship, and we have every intention of succeeding and doing it well. Then life shows up. Time passes, and the fervency we once felt for what we committed ourselves to begins to wane. We find excuses for why we cannot finish what we started.

We've even learned how to spiritualize our excuses for why it's okay for us to quit. We don't want to look unspiritual, so we say things like, "I just don't have a peace about it. God is leading me in another direction." These rationales tend to strip us of perseverance and rob us of victories, breakthroughs, and the capability for excellence in all we do!

Not so with the church in Thyatira. They were fighting the good fight of faith. They were running strongly the race set before them, and they were doing it with excellence.

Even still, there were a few things they were lacking. According to the Son of God, they had allowed this woman Jezebel or people with the same spirit Jezebel had to come in and deceive and mislead those who were following Christ.

The Old Testament character named Jezebel was a woman of royal descent in Phoenicia. She was a prophetess of the false god named Baal! Ahab, who was then king of Israel, fell in love with Jezebel and made her his queen. However, Jezebel had intentions and visions of doing things in Israel that would lead this chosen nation away from Jehovah. She was a woman who was controlling and manipulative, seductive and immoral. Whatever she had to do to get her way, she would do it.

Rather than being an anointed leader and man of God, Ahab allowed her to advance her beliefs and lead Israel into idolatry, sexual practices, and perversions that God had strictly forbidden. She stood opposed to everything Jehovah had proclaimed to His people and even had the prophets of God put to death.

So commanding was Jezebel's influence and control that even the great prophet Elijah ran away and hid in a cave when he first heard of what she had in mind to do concerning the prophets of God!

How easily it seems the people of God can be detoured, distracted, or bullied into places of inaction for the cause of Christ. We hide out in our church buildings because the world outside is just too threatening! The church ends up being bullied into a corner by a culture that does not fear God.

The influence of sin in our society seems so overwhelming, intimidating, and disconcerting that many great men and women of God find it easier to do nothing and say nothing because of the risk of being labeled intolerant or close-minded. Christians who should be standing strong and speaking the truth are much more content to remain secluded in the caves of our churches rather than be the ones who go forward into the darkness with the light of the Truth. Jesus said, "I am the Way, the Truth, and the Life" (John 14:6 NKJV).

Today the church is supposed to be the light of the world.

If we are hiding the truth from the world because of what others might say or think about us, then we are ashamed of the one who is the truth! If we are ashamed of Jesus, then He will be ashamed of us when we stand before the Father, according to Luke 9:26. We cannot hide the truth because of fear or persecution. It is the truth that sets people free from deception and the bondages of sin! The darkness of our world should not strike fear in our hearts but should instead renew a passion in us to shine brighter for the cause of Christ.

In this season of history, the body of Christ cannot afford to be ambiguous about the truth in order to be politically correct! As believers, we have a responsibility and a privilege to speak the truth in love so that the Holy Spirit can do His work of drawing all people to Jesus Christ.

I am not talking about a diluted version of the truth in order to make it more palatable to everyone. I make no reference to someone's opinion of what truth is or is not. I am speaking completely about the absolute truth spelled out in the Word of God—the truth of the Father,

Son, and Holy Spirit, the truth that was given under divine inspiration of the Spirit of God.

People of God who have been redeemed and are victorious, hear what the Spirit is saying to us! We must draw close enough to Him so that when He speaks, we hear with clarity and distinction every single word and breath!

Preoccupation will lead us away from God's presence and His voice. Distraction will steer us into deception. It is imperative for us to be waiting anxiously beside Him so we are ready when He reveals His will, His Word, and His timing.

The individuals in the church of Thyatira who were deceiving the believers were compared to this woman Jezebel. Many true believers were being persuaded to forsake the teachings of Jesus Christ and were beginning to follow into idolatry and sexual immorality with the perception that it was all right.

The church in Thyatira, although making great strides for the gospel, was reprimanded because the members were allowing this false teaching to go unchallenged in their midst.

Today the church finds herself in similar situations. Things that once made people blush and turn away are now commonplace and of little or no concern in our world. These same things are sometimes even tolerated in our churches. The idea has saturated our lives that we can allow sinful behaviors, sexual immorality, adultery, fornication, and all sorts of perversions and that there is no consequence or accountability.

We must pay attention to what we allow into our lives through our eyes and ears. Many people believe the lie that they can live however they want and lead lifestyles of sinfulness, thinking they are free and not even realizing they are in bondage.

Think about that for a minute. In this age of enlightenment, knowledge, and enormous amounts of information, we can find ourselves so confused about what is truly right and what is truly wrong that it is difficult to determine whether we are living life right side up or upside down.

Hosea 4:6 (NKJV) reads, "My people are destroyed for lack of knowledge. Because you have rejected knowledge, I also will reject you from being priest for Me; Because you have forgotten the law of your God."

Today we have so much information available to us through modern technology and the Internet that we have a tendency to believe we are the smartest generation that has ever lived. Smartphones, smart cars, and smart computers do not necessarily make us knowledgeable or smarter.

Having an enormous amount of information at our finger tips through the click of a mouse can make us well informed and yet not give us full understanding of truth and wisdom. Everything on the Internet is not true, but everything written in the Word of God is absolute truth. The knowledge addressed in Hosea is a knowledge of the truth, and that is one thing lacking in our society today because so many people have rejected the truth.

In a time when everything seems relative and nothing seems eternal, many have very quickly exchanged the truth for a lie. Multitudes of people have been raised and are now raising another generation to believe that everything is about their pleasure and their comfort here on this earth. The mind-set is as follows: "What is right for you may not be right for me, so don't push your beliefs on me." There is nothing in their lives of eternal value or absolute truth.

Meanwhile, where is the church in just such a time as this? Are those who should be boldly proclaiming this truth simply content to stay in their hideaways in a state of apathy?

We live in a melting pot of false religions and erroneous beliefs. We see it in our communities. We see it on television. We hear it in music, and we are bombarded with it daily. Religions and beliefs that teach differently than the inspired words of God found in the Holy Bible are leading people into lifestyles of idolatry and worshipping gods who do not even exist. There is one Creator and Sustainer of this world. We may not understand Him. We may not be able to wrap our finite minds around all that He is, but He is the only true and living God!

When we allow someone or something to take first place in our lives over this one who created us, then we are living in idolatry. It could be a false god, a wrong belief system, a relationship, money, sports, music, television, and the list could go on and on. Anything you put before God becomes the god of your life, and this is idolatry.

Meanwhile, the church sits back in her comfortable pews, talks about what a shame it is, and seldom speaks the words of life, truth, and freedom that are available to the unbeliever! We come together on Sunday, sing, praise, give a little, hear the Word preached, leave, and quietly go back into our world, unchanged and unchanging.

In remaining silent, we don't understand our own shackles. If we allow deception and false beliefs to continue without confrontation, we are not living in victory but in disobedience and defeat. This is what the Savior was saying to the church in Thyatira.

We can have the best music in our churches, the best preachers in our pulpits. We can do great works of service in the church and in our communities, and we can even be reaching many with the gospel; however, if we allow sin and deception to exist among us, then we don't even realize that we are in bondage.

We can't be overcomers if we are burdened down. We can't be free when we are handcuffed! We can't live victorious if we are allowing ungodly mind-sets, beliefs, and attitudes to remain in us! Permitting ungodly things in the house of God will rob us of our victory and drain us of our strength!

Just as in the New Testament, John the Baptist was the forerunner and the voice of one crying in the wilderness and saying, "There is one who is coming... Behold the Lamb of God who takes away the sins of the world," so the church must be today! In this postmodern world the church must be the John the Baptist in this wilderness speaking the truth and crying out, "There is one who is coming. There is one who is coming. There is one who is coming, and He is coming soon. Behold the King of Kings and Lord of Lords. He is the way, the truth, and the life."

Jezebel was extremely successful in fulfilling her plan of leading the nation of Israel into idolatry and sexual immorality and away from the God of Israel! In the same way right now as you read this, the Enemy of our souls is also being extremely successful by incarcerating men and women, teenagers and children in thoughts and actions that lead to sin and separation from God.

Second Timothy 3:5–7 warns us,

> But know this, that in the last days perilous times will come: For men will be lovers of themselves, lovers of money, boasters, proud, blasphemers, disobedient to parents, unthankful, unholy, unloving, unforgiving, slanderers, without self-control, brutal, despisers of good, traitors, headstrong, haughty, lovers of pleasure rather than lovers of God, having a form of godliness but denying its power. And from such people turn away! For of this sort are those who creep into households and make captives of gullible women loaded down with sins, led away by various lusts, always learning and never able to come to the knowledge of the truth.

In America there seems to be a spirit of sexual immorality and perversion that has been unleashed into our cities, and too often we are giving this spirit access to our lives and our children by what comes into our homes through different types of media. We may think none of this has an effect on us, but every bit of information that enters our minds through our eyes and ears will have an impact on our actions. This is why there is such an increase in illicit things (adultery, affairs, teenagers and children involved in sexual acts, pornography, and more). Our culture has raised a generation of people who are seemingly out of touch with reality and insensitive to the consequences of their actions and behaviors.

Our minds are the battlegrounds where Satan wages war against our hearts and our souls. This is the reason we are admonished in Scripture to guard our hearts and minds in Christ Jesus. The Enemy cares nothing about you. He just wants to destroy what is important to God.

You are important to God. You are God's highest creation, made in His image, and He loves you with an infinite love! If Satan can destroy you by deceiving you or capturing your mind in a prison of pornography or pushing you into an affair that will destroy your family, then he will do it just to get back at God! It is a trap, and he will steal your victory and eventually your soul.

First Corinthians 6:18–20 (NKJV) tells us,

> Flee sexual immorality. Every sin that a man does is outside the body, but he who commits sexual immorality sins against his own body. Or do you not know that your body is the temple of the Holy Spirit who is in you, whom you have from God, and you are not your own? For you were bought at a price; therefore glorify God in your body and in your spirit, which are God's.

Today the presence of God is no longer confined to a building or a room. Did you get what the Scripture said? "Your body is the temple of the Holy Spirit!" *Wow!* The Holy Spirit of God chooses you and me as His residence. God created you, your body, your mind, your heart, and your spirit as a dwelling place for Himself!

You have a divine purpose and design. God created you just the way you are for His own purpose because you are to be His perfect temple. Therefore, since we have been bought and redeemed with so high a price (the crucifixion, the death, and the resurrection of Jesus Christ), we must live up to the purpose for which we were created.

Unfortunately many times we fall short of achieving that purpose because just like the people of Jesus' day, we allow things to come into our lives that dilute and distort the pure, holy dwelling place we are supposed to be and where God is supposed to reign.

We might think it is nothing, but anytime we compromise, it *is* something! When we do this, we lose! We turn the temple of God into something that He never desired it to be.

If we allow sin into our lives, it will vandalize the property of God! I am not just talking about what many people think are the *big* sins—adultery, murder, stealing, etc. (although we must understand that there truly are no degrees of sin and that sin is sin whether it is little or big, whether public or private).

Even when we allow unforgiveness to live in our hearts, it is one more vandalizing spree from the Enemy. When we gossip about someone else, the Devil destroys one more wall or one more brick of the temple God built. If we tolerate sin and don't deal with it in our lives, our spirit ends up looking like a neglected, battered, unkempt church where there is no sign or indication of the presence of the Lord. The weeds grow up and choke out the life that should be there. God help us because we were created for so much more!

Like Christ did in the temple, there are times when we need to take a whip and chase those things out of our lives rather than partnering with them and believing everything will be all right. We must set the house of God in order and not indulge anything that would deface or damage our temple!

For example, as the owner of rental properties, I know how disheartening and discouraging it is when a tenant I have allowed and trusted to use my property doesn't take care of what has been entrusted to him or her. There are times when I have returned to properties and found holes in the walls, doors hanging off their hinges, roach infestations, permanent marker all over the walls, and unidentifiable things in the carpet. It is infuriating that someone would so carelessly destroy a property that doesn't belong to them.

Perhaps God feels the same way about our bodies and our lives. First Corinthians 6 tells us that "we are not our own but were bought with a price." God created us, bought us back from sin, and holds full ownership to our temple. He has possession of the deed! So how are we caring for this house of God we live in every day? This temple belongs to Him, and we should glorify Him with how we inhabit it and use it.

If you find yourself in the battle of pornography or immorality, it is destroying the temple, and the only way to have victory is to throw yourself on the mercy seat of God and allow Him to cleanse, purify, and remodel your temple! How do you do that?

Look what Romans 12:1–2 (NLT) says,

> And so, dear brothers and sisters, I plead with you to give your bodies to God because of all he has done for you. Let them be a living and holy sacrifice—the kind he will find acceptable. This is truly the way to worship him. Don't copy the behavior and customs of this world, but let God transform you into a new person by changing the way you think. Then you will learn to know God's will for you, which is good and pleasing and perfect.

When we truly give ourselves to God as a sacrifice each day, He can and will transform the way we think and act, and our lives will become the pleasing and acceptable temple in which He longs to dwell! It is required that we daily lay our lives on the altar of God in complete surrender and stay there. It is not truly a sacrifice of ourselves if we constantly crawl off the altar and pursue our own ways. When we submit ourselves to the lordship of Christ, God can transform us to become more like Him.

I don't want to come across as though this is a magical wand God waves and *poof* all your issues with these things are gone. Most of the time it is a process we must walk through. We give ourselves to God; however, we still live in these bodies of flesh and bone, and sometimes the desires of this flesh can come back with a vengeance. In the moments when they do, we must respond exactly the way 2 Corinthians 10:4–6 tells us.

> For the weapons of our warfare are not carnal but mighty in God for pulling down strongholds, casting down arguments and every high thing that exalts itself against the knowledge of God, bringing every thought into captivity to the obedience of Christ, and being ready to punish all disobedience when your obedience is fulfilled.

When those thoughts and desires present themselves, we must act immediately and snatch them out of the air and bring them under subjection to Jesus Christ. We should not try to hide them from Him. He already knows us perfectly! We should give them all to Him, get into His Word, and let His Word get into us, and we will walk as an overcomer second by second, moment by moment, and day by day! If we mess up and fall, we must get back up, dust ourselves off, come in repentance, and set our eyes back on Jesus!

There is a consequence for those who allow this type of sin to permeate their lives. The Lord tells the church at Thyatira that there will be tribulation and sickness and eventually death to the offspring of the influences of Jezebel. Those who are led away into this lifestyle of sin and idolatry will experience death.

Although there are times that physical disease and death accompany this lifestyle and are the consequences of the choices people make, the reality of this sickness and death is not necessarily so much physical as it is spiritual. A spiritual death is far more terminal than a physical death.

There is a reward for those who take hold of the truth and get victory over sin. The Lord promises that He will put no other burden upon us if we hold fast to the conquest that He has already given us!

We are assured of power and authority with Christ! The rod mentioned in Revelation 2:27 is symbolic of power and authority. Christ, having been given the nations by the Father, will rule them with total and absolute authority. To rule with a rod of iron does not mean that we will have a brutal rule or that He will be an oppressive tyrant but that He will rule with an authority that will forever be immovable, unchallenged, and invincible.

The one who overcomes in this life will be given the power and authority to rule with Christ when He comes again! If we remain strong and true and hold fast to what He has given us, we will share in His kingdom! The old kingdoms and influences of this world will be done away with and broken under the reign of Christ so that He can make all things new under His authority.

Revelation 2:28 says, "And I will give him the Morning Star." There are times in the Bible when Jesus is referred to as the Morning Star (Revelation 22:16) or the Day Star (2 Peter 1:19)! Since we live in the darkness of this world, what greater blessing could there be than to have His light to show us the way! Darkness can never eclipse the Morning Star. The night will never extinguish the light of the Morning Star.

Just as the final moments of night lose their grip on darkness, the Morning Star begins to shine through, and it is a whole new day, a whole new dawning of hope and possibility, a brand-new trusting in the faithfulness of God, whose mercies become new every morning!

Forget about the success or failures of the battles you fought yesterday and see what new mercies shine through when the Morning Star arises in your life! Those who overcome will be given the Morning Star, and He will light their way. They will no longer stumble around in darkness. He will bring them from victory to victory!

In your personal life you may feel as though you are daily bombarded with thoughts, desires, or visual images that attempt to seduce you to sin. Temptation may seem to be around every corner you turn. It may appear there is no escape, but *there is hope!*

You can overcome through the power of the Holy Spirit that lives within you. You don't have to be swayed and influenced by a culture whose sole purpose seems to be an attempt to steal your purity and your life in Christ. Don't allow immoral or improper thoughts to imprison your mind. Take your eyes off the things that so easily drag you down and walk away from them step by step as you are led by the presence of God. Hold fast and firm to the things the Spirit of God has placed within you through His Word. He has created you as His temple, so glorify Him in your body, mind, heart, and spirit! Remember, "'It's not by your might nor by your power, but by my Spirit,' says the Lord" (Zechariah 4:6).

~

I, Jesus, have sent My angel to testify to you these things in the churches. I am the Root and the Offspring of David, the Bright and Morning Star. And the Spirit and the bride say, "Come!" And let him who hears say, "Come!" And let him who thirsts come. Whoever desires, let him take the water of life freely.

—Revelation 22:16–17 (NKJV)

CHAPTER 6

Come Alive and Pay Attention! Church of Sardis

And to the angel of the church in Sardis write, "These things says He who has the seven Spirits of God and the seven stars: 'I know your works, that you have a name that you are alive, but you are dead. Be watchful, and strengthen the things which remain, that are ready to die, for I have not found your works perfect before God. Remember therefore how you have received and heard; hold fast and repent. Therefore if you will not watch, I will come upon you as a thief, and you will not know what hour I will come upon you. You have a few names even in Sardis who have not defiled their garments; and they shall walk with Me in white, for they are worthy. He who overcomes shall be clothed in white garments, and I will not blot out his name from the Book of Life; but I will confess his name before My Father and before His angels. He who has an ear, let him hear what the Spirit says to the churches.'"

—Revelation 3:1–6 (NKJV)

The city of Sardis was a city set on a hill and extremely fortified yet not impenetrable. It was a city with a rich heritage, a place of wealth and reputation. At one time it had been the capital of the kingdom of Lydia, but a lot had changed in Sardis.

As this Word comes from the Savior, the one who has the seven spirits of God and the seven stars, Sardis finds herself in a place of decision. Although the city of Sardis is not noted to have been the habitation of a specific evil or a throne of Satan or the depths of Satan or to even have its liars or Jezebels or Balaams, there was still a very serious issue happening in this once great city.

The one who holds the seven spirits, representing the Holy Spirit of God and the works and ministries He does in the lives of believers (see Isaiah 11:2–5), and the seven stars, which represent the seven churches, has a message aimed directly at this church and every believer both then and now. The Son of God is the one who sent the Holy Spirit, and He is the one who controls the church. He sends His Spirit where He desires, and He does in His church what he desires. The Holy Spirit flows through a church or individual when He is sent by the Word of God!

Jesus knew the works of this church, and He knew even those things they were hiding that no one else was able to see or discern. We might think we can hide things from God, but there is nothing hidden from His eyes. Hebrews 4:13 (NIV) discloses this truth when it says, "Nothing in all creation is hidden from God's sight. Everything is uncovered and laid bare before the eyes of Him to whom we must give account."

According to Revelation 3:1 this church in Sardis had a name that they were alive, but the reality was they were dead. In the eyes of mankind they were vibrant and full of life, but in the eyes of God they had ceased to exist or fulfill their purpose.

From all outward appearances it looked as if everything in the church of Sardis was going well. They had a reputation from what they used to be. They were living life on that reputation.

Reputation can be an interesting and important thing because it can either make you a legend or it can destroy your life. Think of what reputation has done in the lives of many individuals over the years.

It has caused people to perceive men like Chuck Norris as invincible and all-powerful in the eyes of those who believe the quotes about Him. His history as a tough fighter and actor who plays in "tough guy" roles has given him a reputation and following. Let me just say that I love the quotes about Chuck Norris. For instance, "Chuck Norris and Superman once fought each other on a bet. The loser had to start wearing his underwear on the outside of his pants." "Chuck Norris has a grizzly bear carpet in his room. The bear is not dead. It is just afraid to move." "Chuck Norris died twenty years ago. Death just hasn't built up the courage to tell him yet." I love it!

Still, for all those to whom reputation has been a great thing, there are many more for whom reputation has been their nemesis.

Will reputation be an architect and builder in your life, or will it be a demolition crew? The choices we make in our lives and the actions and words that accompany those decisions will help others formulate an opinion in their minds about who and what we are. What is the reputation you want the world to see in your life? Are your choices, words, and actions feeding that reputation? Although the reputation of this church was a good one, they were not living up to the merits of their reputation when this letter was written.

There have been so many times in my ministry when people have recounted to me how God has previously worked in their lives and their churches. I've heard stories of how a particular church had grown and experienced revival through a sovereign move of God. I have also heard descriptions of how God once did miracles and how the power and presence of God used to be incredible.

Let me say that there is nothing wrong with remembrance. Calling those things of the *past* to our minds to stir us and prompt us to go forward *now* can be very beneficial. There are times when we need to remember the past so that it can guide our future.

However, it is never a healthy thing to live in the past, whether good or bad, because it can become a detriment to the present! God cannot do in you today and tomorrow what He wants if you are constantly looking back at the past.

We wouldn't think about getting in our vehicles and driving down the road with our heads turned backward and looking at where we've been. Why not? Because that kind of driving is reckless and irresponsible and leads to an imminent collision. Why do we try to maneuver our spiritual lives that way? It will only lead to disaster, defeat, and disillusionment!

It would seem the church in Sardis, although activities were happening and good things were going on, was riding on the past and the reputation of what used to be much like some do today. Looking at them from the outside, someone might say they were alive, but in seeing them through the eyes of the Spirit, it appeared that death was all around.

There was no true life or power in what they were doing. What was once alive and vibrant in this church was now nothing more than an extinguished fire and a decaying corpse.

From my perspective this seems to be a prevalent issue in Christianity today. There is the appearance of life, but it is nothing more than a facade of spirituality. Many can recall when they came into relationship with the Lord and can passionately tell you what they thought in that moment of giving their lives to the Savior. The exhilaration they felt when their sins were forgiven was incredible, but they never grow and mature in their walk with Christ past that moment. When we are not growing and changing, we are dying.

This is a frightening neighborhood to live in because in this place our walk with Christ becomes what the Bible refers to in 2 Timothy 3:5 (NKJV) as "having a form of godliness but denying its power." When we live in this place of death, what used to be a dwelling place for the power and presence of the Holy Spirit is turned into a place of religiosity and ritual devoid of any life. It becomes a place of activity rather than a place of anointing. It doesn't matter what the outward appearance may be, we become desolate on the inside. You can dress it up and call it whatever you want, but at the end of the day death is still death!

This principle is somewhat like a puppet. As long as the hand of the puppeteer is in the puppet, that puppet becomes alive. It moves and speaks as the puppeteer directs it. Yet as soon as the hand of the puppeteer is removed from the puppet, there is no longer life in it. Regardless of how beautiful the puppet may be or how alive it may appear, without the puppeteer it is lifeless. This is how the church is when we become devoid of the hand and power of the Holy Spirit. When He directs our lives, actions, and words, there is abundant life, but when His hand is removed from our lives, we are lifeless and empty no matter what we may look like on the outside.

We have to remember that God looks at the heart according to 1 Samuel 16:7, which says, "But the LORD said to Samuel, 'Do not look at his appearance or at his physical stature, because I have refused him. For the LORD does not see as man sees; for man looks at the outward appearance, but the LORD looks at the heart.'"

This is why when Jesus spoke to the scribes and Pharisees in Matthew 23:27 (NJKV). He said, "Woe to you, scribes and Pharisees, hypocrites! For you are like whitewashed tombs which indeed appear beautiful outwardly, but inside are full of dead men's bones and all uncleanness."

At times we tend be more concerned about what men think and see (reputation) rather than what God sees and knows (reality)! Someone may have the reputation among men of being the most spiritual person in the world, but what does God see when He looks past all the decorations and activities of the person's life and focuses in on his heart? Is it still beating? Is there still life? Is the man's heart still loving Him?

According to J. Hampton Keathley, III, in his commentary on the message to Sardis, "The two life-giving provisions of God for man—the Holy Spirit and the Word—were being neglected. The result was spiritual deadness." Anytime we allow the Word of God and the Spirit of God to become neglected or take a backseat in our lives, the result is always spiritual death. We are no longer moved by the Word or lead by the Spirit.

In comparison, when a gardener prunes a plant, the pruning is healthy for the plant, but what happens to those branches and leaves that are removed from the plant? Because they are no longer connected to their source of life and nutrition, they shrivel up, dry out, and die. The nutrients that once coursed through those now detached areas and brought health to those parts of the plant are no longer flowing because they have been disconnected from the provision. As they lay detached on the ground, the sun may still shine on those branches, and they may still get soaked in the rain; however, this doesn't ensure their health and life! We will only have life and growth in the Lord when we remain attached and sensitive to His Word and His Spirit!

Allow me to share a secret with you. Satan loves a dead church. He loves it when a church *looks* as though it is alive. However, the reality of that church is that its heart stopped beating long ago and no one is doing CPR. Why does he love that? Because it is the Enemy's passion and purpose to steal, kill, and destroy, and if he can bring churches or individuals to the place where they are living in the past and what used to be, then he can cut them off and steal their nourishment.

If they are functioning on reputation rather than the Spirit of God, he can stop the pulse of God in that church and destroy the vehicle of the message of the gospel. This is his ultimate motivation—to stop the life-changing message and salvation of the gospel.

If we allow him to, he will deprive churches of any fresh revelation from God and steal their relevancy in the world today!

It is time for the people of God to allow the Spirit and the Word to break out the spiritual AED (automated electronic defibrillator), shout, "Clear," and spark some new, real, and vibrant life into the church. Shock us, Holy Spirit, until the heart of the church is beating once again with the heartbeat of Jesus!

This church is instructed to "be watchful and strengthen the things which remain, that are ready to die" (Revelation 3:2). Lying dormant beneath all the activities and programs and supposed signs of life, under the reality of impending death, there must have been some small, seemingly insignificant remembrance of what was pure and holy.

There must have been at least a small morsel of morality and breath that remained but was losing its fight with death. The Spirit speaks to this tiny tidbit. The Spirit breathes His words of life to this small remnant, which have not defiled their garments, and He says, "Awaken. Come back to life. Be strengthened and sustained."

Just as Jesus called Lazarus back from a place of death and new life was born in him, so the Spirit is calling His church. Will the church hear the utterance of the Spirit of God and respond?

In this world of death and destruction, where it seems every bit of morality and purity has been stripped away, the remnant of those who truly love Christ can become overwhelmed with the magnitude of trying to live lives of purity and remain true.

It seems as though spiritual death is breathing down the neck of the church, and so many who once claimed the name of Christ have given up the fight for life and succumbed to this death, being content rather to just *do* the Christian activities and *appear* holy without the life-giving power of the Word and the Spirit.

For those who have not given in and perhaps for those who have given in and seen the need for revival, the Spirit says, "Be watchful... come back to life... and strengthen those things which remain" (Revelation 3:2).

There is an urgency in His words because of the discernment of what spiritual death brings to an individual or a church! We must do it *now*. There is no time to wait. Death stands at the door, and if we permit him entrance, he will steal everything Christ came to give us! The life more abundantly that is promised to every believer will be turned into a valley of dry bones!

Death can steal our eternity with the one who loved us so much that He gave Himself to redeem us and bring us to this life. Even if there is the smallest shred of love, hope, purity, or faith, it *must* be strengthened, and it *must* be done now. If not, death will be the result.

It doesn't take a lot of faith to move mountains. In Matthew 17:20 (NKJV), Jesus said to them, "I say to you, if you have faith as a mustard seed, you will say to this mountain, 'Move from here to there,' and it will move; and nothing will be impossible for you."

Do you know how small a mustard seed is? They are tiny, usually about one to two millimeters in diameter, and yet with so little faith, we can move spiritual mountains out of our way.

We all want to be strong in our faith. We look at men like Abraham or David and think, *If I could just have faith like they did, I could win. I could slay this giant in my life.* Here is a dose of truth: Even the smallest fragment of faith can do mighty works in the life of a believer.

When we start with small faith and win a victory, it is exercising and strengthening our faith for the next assault.

When a man makes up his mind to become a bodybuilder, that person doesn't start out with bulging muscles and incredible strength the first time he steps into the gym. Instead, he may walk in as a 150-pound, soaking wet weakling. He may walk out of the first visit to that gym weak and tired and sore, but if he sticks with it, pushes and pulls the weights to and from his body, endures the soreness and torn muscles, eventually those muscles will heal and get bigger. They will gain size, strength, and endurance. It is the same with our faith.

If we don't use it, then our faith will become weak and flabby! But if we set our minds and our sights on obtaining the victory through faith, we will see it! "Faith is the confidence that what we hope for will actually happen; it gives us assurance about things we cannot see" (Hebrews 11:1 NLT).

During your struggle you may come to a point where you feel like you do not have much left to offer God, but if you will hear what the Spirit is saying and strengthen those little things that do remain, He will bring you to an unimaginable life of victory!

God will pour out faith and strength into your heart and spirit, and you will arise to go forward another day! The endurance and triumph you had hoped for will become a reality in your life.

So how do you strengthen those things that remain when you don't even feel you have enough strength to utter a prayer? You must allow the Spirit of God to bring the strength. That's why it tells us in Zechariah 4:6 (NKJV), "It's not by might, nor by power, but by my Spirit says the Lord."

We can't do it on our own, and this fact is where most people get into trouble. We want to do it by our own agenda rather than allowing the Spirit of God to do it His way. But we cannot bring life to our own spirit. Life only comes from the Spirit of God!

At the moment you were conceived in your mother's womb, it wasn't you who brought life to yourself. In reality, it wasn't even your mom and dad who brought life to you. God gave you life. Your parents' DNA may have come together, but it is God who provides the life in every instance!

When we come in true repentance and absolute surrender, the Spirit revives us, refills us, refreshes us, renews us, empowers us, and gives us life!

The flip side to this scenario brings us to the stern warning of God to this church. If we allow things to continue as they are until even the embers of godliness that remain are snuffed out, then He will come upon us as a thief, and we won't even know when He is coming.

What does a thief do?

A thief comes in and takes away those things that are valuable to you. The things you treasure he claims for his own.

Consider what was apparently valuable to this church in Sardis. Their reputation, their good name, and their appearance of godliness were their treasures. God sent a warning saying that He would come in and take that away and remove from them the things they considered valuable because they did not value the life they could have in Him.

Reputation had become more important to them than relationship!

Are there things in your life that once were a raging fire for God and now are just smoldering embers about to go out? Have you permitted possessions or reputation to become of greater value to you than a deep, intimate relationship with your Creator? Are you content to just have a form of godliness or a reputation of spirituality and yet inside be filled with dead bones? The Spirit is calling you back to life!

Like the very dry bones resting in the valley, which Elijah saw in the vision he received from the Lord, you, too, can come back to real life (Ezekiel 37:1-4). These bones were the remnants of an army who had lost the war, and their carcasses were left in the valley to be devoured by wild animals and scorched by the sun. When Elijah was shown this scene, it was utter devastation and complete lifelessness. There was nothing left. Have you ever felt like you've been there? I've walked in that valley a number of times myself.

When the Word of God went out to those bones, their status could not remain the same! Death could not hold onto his grip of those bones. They began to move and shake and come back together piece by piece, but still the picture was not complete.

They may have been perfect skeletal specimens, but God wasn't finished with them yet. His work in them would not be complete until they were whole again.

The Almighty spoke through Elijah again, causing muscles and tendons to be layered over those bones, and skin began to stretch out and cover them. Although they lay there now as full-bodied people, still there was no life in them!

God used Elijah one more time to speak to the wind, and the wind (the breath of the Spirit of God) filled their nostrils and lungs. They became alive and stood up on their feet!

The valley, which once had been a testimony of the Enemy's power of death, now became an incredible praise report of God's life-giving power.

Situations that seem hopeless to us are simply opportunities for God to do the miraculous. Our test will become our testimony.

Regardless of how many battles you may have lost or how much territory you may have surrendered to the Enemy, God can restore life to you if you will hear what the Spirit is saying. Let Him speak until you feel it all the way to your bones!

The Bible is full of promises God has made to His children, and God is faithful to fulfill every one of His promises.

I love the covenant the Spirit spoke to this church in Sardis. "The one who overcomes will walk with Him in white for they will be worthy" (Revelation 3:4 NKJV). White represents purity and worthiness! Just as a bride on her wedding day wears a beautiful white gown that has been made and tailored to fit only her, so those who overcome and are the bride of Christ will be clothed in white garments to show the purity of Christ in us. These gowns will be tailor-made specifically for the ones who overcome.

With garments not spoiled by the sin and idols and false beliefs of man, we will be attired in purity and holiness. This will be a fashion statement to end all fashion statements! None of the fine clothing and designers who are popular today could even begin to compare!

When we walk as overcomers by the grace of God and do not allow ourselves to become corrupted with the mind-sets, perceptions, and reputations of this world, then this faith is accounted to us as righteousness, and it makes us worthy through His Spirit to be numbered with the ones who will wear white on that day, pure and holy in His sight.

Keeping ourselves alive in this instance has nothing to do with a survival mentality. It has to do with approaching every day with the mind-set of a conqueror. It means keeping our hearts steadfast in the Word and our spirits in sync with the Spirit of God.

No more living on yesterday's victory. No more relying on a powerful move of God from two years ago. *This* is our day to come back to life, and when we do, we will walk in an abundant life

The message to the church in Sardis goes on to tell us, "He will not blot out your name from the book of life but will confess your name before the Father" (Revelation 3:5 NKJV).

There are two important things going on here. First when we find our lives in Him and continue in Him, our names are secure in the Book of Life. Secondly He will acknowledge us as one of His own before His Father.

This Book of Life seems to be a catalogue of names of those who will live eternally with God. Only God has access to this book, and so He is the only one who can add or delete names from this book. This gives hope and assurance to those who are in Christ that when we suffer or fight or grieve or are tempted and we hold on to our relationship with God and never compromise, our place in eternity with Him will never be removed or erased. Our names will not be blotted out.

We also have to consider the ramifications of this statement. Does this statement also bring with it the idea that it is possible for a name to be blotted out of the Book of Life and someone's eternity with God jeopardized or completely lost? I believe so!

Unless we continue to walk in the Word and in the Spirit, we will find ourselves living in the place of death. In John 15:4–6 (NKJV), Jesus states,

> Abide in Me, and I in you. As the branch cannot bear fruit of itself, unless it abides in the vine, neither can you, unless you abide in Me. I am the vine, you are the branches. He who abides in Me, and I in him, bears much fruit; for without Me you can do nothing. If anyone does not abide in Me, he is cast out as a branch and is withered; and they gather them and throw them into the fire, and they are burned.

These words of Christ give us an understanding of the importance of remaining in Him because He is our source of life. If we do not abide in Him, then we are cut off and removed from the eternal life we have been promised. When we do not live in purity, holiness, and victory, *we* remove the promise from our lives, *not* God.

This Scripture seems to confirm the belief that our names can be removed from the Book of Life if we do not stay in relationship with Jesus. Our Lord did not come to earth, live, die, and rise again for us to live comfortably in the place of death. He came to bring life.

If we compromise the life we have in Him for the things of this world, our names will be removed from the Book of Life. We must stir up the flames and revive those things that are about to die.

In other words, we can't live in sin, complacency, or impurity and expect God to be all right with it! He calls us to life and holiness. When we continue in those things, our names will never be removed. What a comfort that is to those who are fighting the good fight of faith and pressing through to victory!

You may never see your name in lights on a Broadway marquee. Your name may never scroll in the credits of a blockbuster hit movie. Your name may never grace the cover of *Vogue* or *PEOPLE Magazine.* But if your name is written in God's Book of Life, it is more valuable and eternal than being listed with rulers, kings, celebrities, or presidents!

On the day you walk with Him in white, Jesus will stand before the throne of the Father, and in the presence of all the angelic beings who cry out, "Holy, holy, holy," around the throne of God, He will point to you and say, "This one belongs with us."

Can you hear what the Spirit of God is breathing to His church? He loves His children and desires to be with you for eternity. He will give you strength to overcome, and you will sit with Him in heavenly places!

~

The thief does not come except to steal, and to kill,
and to destroy. I have come that they may have life,
and that they may have it more abundantly.

—John 10:10 (NKJV)

CHAPTER 7

I Am Weak... But He Is Strong! Church of Philadelphia

And to the angel of the church in Philadelphia write, "These things says He who is holy, He who is true, He who has the key of David, He who opens and no one shuts, and shuts and no one opens 'I know your works. See, I have set before you an open door, and no one can shut it; for you have a little strength, have kept My word, and have not denied My name. Indeed I will make those of the synagogue of Satan, who say they are Jews and are not, but lie—indeed I will make them come and worship before your feet, and to know that I have loved you. Because you have kept My command to persevere, I also will keep you from the hour of trial which shall come upon the whole world, to test those who dwell on the earth. Behold, I am coming quickly! Hold fast what you have, that no one may take your crown. He who overcomes, I will make him a pillar in the temple of My God, and he shall go out no more. I will write on him the name of My God and the name of the city of My God, the New Jerusalem, which comes down out of heaven

from My God. And I will write on him My new name. He who
has an ear, let him hear what the Spirit says to the churches.'"

—Revelation 3:7–13 (NKJV)

Philadelphia was a city in Lydia whose name meant "brotherly
love." This city was known as a gateway to the east, and out of its
agricultural and trade success, prosperity had come. It was nicknamed
"Little Athens" because of the many temples and shrines present in
the city. The city of Philadelphia and surrounding areas often had
earthquakes and could be an unstable place to live. This church would
have understood the nuances of this message from the Lord that might
seem a little cloudy to us today.

The Lord Himself is identified as speaking to the church within
Philadelphia because Jesus Christ is the one who is known as being
holy and true.

Numerous Scriptures, including Acts 4:27 and 1 John 5:20, reiterate
the absoluteness that Jesus is holy and true. Even the unclean spirit
that Jesus was casting out of a man in Mark 1:24 identified Jesus as
"the Holy One of God."

Many times what we believe and appropriate into our lives will
depend on what we know about the history, reputation, and character
of the one who is speaking to us! If we know that Jesus is holy and
true, then we will also know that we can trust Him and embrace what
He says. Jesus is holy and true in every word, every action, and every
attribute of who He is. In Him there is nothing unholy, dishonest, or
false.

We may understand the holy and true part, but we might say,
"What in the world does He mean when He says, 'He who has the key of
David, He who opens and no one shuts, and shuts and no one opens'?"

The key of David refers to King David, and it gives the impression
of one who has the ultimate authority.

In my research I found this information from an unknown source, which helped unpack this phrase to me. In Luke 24:27 the Bible reads concerning Jesus, "And beginning at Moses and all the Prophets, He expounded to them in all the Scriptures the things concerning Himself."

According to this passage of Scripture, while He was walking on the road to Emmaus with two of His disciples after His resurrection, Jesus told them every place in Scripture throughout the Old Testament where He could be found.

He was there in every foreshadowing, every type, and every figure. All the way from Moses and throughout all the prophets, the Lord is shown! From Abraham's intent and act of offering Isaac in worship to Hosea redeeming his wayward wife, Gomer, we see the foretelling and attributes of the Lamb of God, who takes away the sins of the world.

Scripture is replete with prophecy concerning Jesus Christ. As the Lord walked with these two men on the road to Emmaus, He communicated this to them clearly so there would be no mistaking who He truly was.

This previous phrase concerning the key of David is a quote from Isaiah 22:22 (NKJV), which says, "The key of the house of David I will lay on his shoulder; So he shall open, and no one shall shut; And he shall shut, and no one shall open."

This was written in reference to a man named Eliakim, who was the son of Hilkiah. Eliakim would be given the authority that would come with the key of David! We know from the genealogy of Jesus in Matthew 1 that Jesus was descended from the line of David and as such would have the right to hold the key of David and have the authority of the throne of David!

It is no coincidence that the name Eliakim literally translates as "Resurrection of God" and that the name Hilkiah translates as "Portion of Yah (God)." Both names are pointing again to Jesus Christ.

The only person who can unlock and open the door is the one with the key, the one who was and is and always will be! When He shuts a door, it remains shut, and when He opens a door, it remains open.

This is a good lesson for us to learn in light of who Jesus is in our lives. Many times out of our own personal agendas, we try to either kick down doors that He has shut or slam shut doors that He has opened that are not to our liking. When we surrender the lordship of our lives to Him, we give Him the key and full authority!

Therefore, the question is this: What does it mean for Him to have full authority in our lives?

Well, think of it this way: If I give you a key to my house, what is my implication in doing that? With a key you now have entrance into my home, my life, and my family. You can come and go at my house whenever you like. You have complete access!

If Jesus has the key of our lives, then we have given Him the right to come in and have full access and full authority. If He wants to lock a door, then we let Him. If He wants to unlock and swing wide the door, then He can!

If we believe that He is holy and true, then when He shuts a door, we need to trust Him and let it stay shut, and when He opens a door, we need to walk through it in full faith and obedience!

Alexander Graham Bell said, "Sometimes we stare so long at a door that is closing that we see too late the one that is open."

I'm reminded of Genesis 7, where God told Noah to build an ark. Noah did as the Lord commanded, and when the ark was complete, Noah and his family boarded along with all the animals that God had told him to bring into the ark. When everyone was aboard, verse 16 says, "And the Lord shut him in."

When the Lord shut the door of the ark, it meant that no one else was allowed to enter. Only those of faith who had believed the Word of God were allowed to embark, and when God shut that door, no one could open it! It probably was very difficult for Noah and his family to hear his former neighbors and friends banging on the ark and screaming for mercy, knowing there was nothing they could do to change the situation because God had sealed the doorway.

Nevertheless, though they may have been saddened by the fate of those who did not believe, do you know what that shut door on the ark meant to Noah and his family? It meant that God had spared them. God had protected them. God had preserved them.

Because God shut that door, they would not drown and be swept away in the flood. In His awesome providence, God was safeguarding them against His judgment and destruction.

Sometimes we need to just let shut doors remain shut even if they are not doors we wanted God to shut. It might just be God's way of protecting us.

Because He holds the key of ultimate authority in our lives, we must trust that every closed door is His wisdom and protection and every open door is His providence and blessing, whether they appear to be that way or not.

This is where faith and trust come into the equation. Are we going to trust God even though we don't understand why He has closed this door and opened another? Are we going to have faith in Him even though He answered our prayer in a way we didn't envision or expect?

The church in Philadelphia had been faithful to God, and the congregation was the only church to receive complete commendation from the Lord. He told them, as He had the other churches, "I know your works." As stated before, the fact that God knows our works and actions even when we think no one else knows can be intimidating, but when we have been wholly faithful, those words are a comfort and a joy!

When we know our lives have been pleasing to God, we want Him to take notice of us. When a child first learns to do something new, like a cartwheel, what is the first thing the parents are going to hear? "Look, Mom. Look, Dad. See what I can do! Mom and Dad, watch me." And guess what the parents will do? They will watch their child as he or she cartwheels over and over and over again and tell their kid what a great job he or she has done and how proud they are of the child. When a child receives acclamation and applause, it lights a fire in his or her eyes to see what else he or she can do to get your approval!

There is nothing that escapes the eyes of God! Whether bad or good, He sees, and He knows! Like a teenage boy who has cleaned his room without his parents asking him to, the Christian who is faithful doesn't have to worry when God says, "I know what you've done!"

Although the church in Philadelphia had little strength, which could mean they were small in number or that their strength had been exhausted during the course of their walk with Christ and only a little remained, still He compliments and encourages them because they have kept His Word and not denied His name. The image here is of a church that loved Jesus Christ with everything in it and would never back down. Even though they were tired, worn out, and beat up, they never let go of what He had spoken to them and done in their lives.

This is critical to our living victoriously in Christ! Oftentimes in the newness and excitement of salvation, we promise the Lord that we will live for Him forever! We declare that we will never forsake Him, but in the course of our busy lives or in the face of persecution or ridicule or fear or sickness, we don't cling to that promise.

There is a picture that has become a famous icon of the spirit of America. After the terrorist attacks in the Unites States on September 11, 2001, a candid photo was taken of three New York firefighters raising the banner of this nation, the American flag. Surrounded by absolute devastation and death, they painstakingly raised that flag to symbolize and show the world that no matter what assault or ambush we face as a nation, we would forever stand strong and true.

Don't let the battles in your life command what your response will be. You may feel like sitting down and weeping. You may even feel emotionally, mentally, and physically distraught. Searching the horizon, you may not find any glimmers of hope, but you muster the strength to lift up your banner of faith and press through! The attack won't last forever, and God is with you!

In Luke 22:31–34 (NKJV), the Bible says,

> And the Lord said, "Simon, Simon! Indeed, Satan has asked for you, that he may sift you as wheat. But I have prayed for you, that your faith should not fail; and when you have returned to Me, strengthen your

brethren." But he said to Him, "Lord, I am ready to go with You, both to prison and to death." Then He said, "I tell you, Peter, the rooster shall not crow this day before you will deny three times that you know Me."

In this moment Peter was telling the Lord that he was drawing a line in the sand and that he was going to stand with Him. He declared that he would never leave Jesus even if it meant imprisonment and death! These were brave words for a man who was not in the heat of battle at the moment!

As the story continues to unfold, we find Jesus arrested, and initially it looked as though Peter would stay true to his words. When the soldiers came to arrest Jesus, Peter drew his sword and cut off the ear of one of the soldiers. Jesus rebuked Peter's actions and healed the man.

"But commitment means staying loyal to what you said you were going to do long after the mood you said it in has left you" (Jonathon Field).

Fast-forward now to the courtyard after Jesus was arrested. Peter was waiting in the courtyard around a fire, and fear set into his heart. After a little time to think this through and process what was happening, fear set in. So crippling was his fear that this man of strong words and actions, when faced with the soldiers, now denied even knowing Christ to a lowly servant girl.

It is interesting how the hearts and minds of men and women who have made a covenant with Jesus can change so quickly. Sometimes in difficulty and sometimes in ease, we forget our vows to the Lord. Sometimes in poverty and sometimes in prosperity we don't remember the promises we made. Whether in fear or in comfort, we can easily forsake our covenant.

This was not so for the church in Philadelphia. Even though their strength was small, they never gave up and never gave in! They held on to the words of Christ and the name of Jesus!

Because of their steadfastness, God opened a door before them. A door that had previously been inaccessible to them God was now swinging wide open for them to walk through. It is quite possible that this door was a gateway to spreading the news of the gospel and increasing the kingdom of God. The way of salvation was thrown open wide to them.

This was a door that no enemy would be able to shut! As they walked through this door, God anointed them and increased their ministry and influence. Because of their perseverance and stamina, the world saw the power of Christ.

We need to get this into our spirit: When God opens a door before us for ministry or service, there is no devil, demon, enemy, government, family member, or friend who can shut it! God places it there for the blessing and provision of those who are faithful to Him. The Enemy cannot steal what God has given you unless you surrender it to him!

I know there is a spiritual warfare going on and Satan is attempting to silence those who proclaim the name of Jesus Christ. He is working overtime to exhaust the body of Christ of their strength, but I also see that God is opening doors to those who have been obedient to Him. God is making a way of provision that previously was not available.

Doors of salvation for spouses, children, and family for whom we have been praying will open quickly. Doors of healing are opening wide! Doors of deliverance are swinging completely open! Doors of opportunity that we didn't even see before are now accessible to us.

Those who used to mock our faith and speak against us will see God's blessing on our lives and will fall down in humility and worship God. Those who once ridiculed us will now be seeking us out and asking us to pray for them.

Don't give up! Even when it seems like all hope is gone and you don't have another ounce of energy with which to step out in faith, keep on stepping.

Scripture says, "My grace is sufficient for you, for My strength is made perfect in weakness. Therefore most gladly I will rather boast in my infirmities, that the power of Christ may rest upon me. Therefore I take pleasure in infirmities, in reproaches, in needs, in persecutions, in distresses for Christ's sake. For when I am weak, then I am strong" (2 Corinthians 12:9–10 NKJV).

I love the promises of God to this faithful church. He reminds them that He is coming quickly and encourages people to hold fast what they have so that no one can take away their crown of life.

This crown of life represents eternal life. How important is eternal life to you? Oftentimes we wholeheartedly strive for and accumulate the possessions and wealth of this world and don't want to let them go. This type of desperation is how we should cling to those things we have in Christ, so that in the end we can hear Him say, "Well done, my good and faithful servant."

Will we still embrace the name of Christ even in a world that is hostile to it? Are we willing to hear the Word of the Lord and be obedient to it even in a world filled with distractions and voices demanding our attention?

Jesus is coming soon, and He is looking for faith and faithfulness. Those who have been counted as faithful He has promised to deliver from the "hour of trial that is to come to the whole world."

There is coming a time on this earth of trial and tribulation, a season when there will be severe persecution, and a day when peace and safety is promised but never delivered. The rise of the Antichrist will usher in an era of evil and destruction such as the world has never known.

It seems the promise of the Savior is that He will deliver His people from this tribulation period so they do not have to go through it but instead will be in His presence forever. For the ones who walk in triumph and rise above the enemies of this world, He will provide a way of escaping the tribulation by returning and claiming us as His own.

To the one who overcomes, He says, "I will make Him a pillar in the temple of my God and He shall go out no more" (Revelation 3:12 NKJV).

A city like Philadelphia, which was plagued with frequent earthquakes, would understand with clarity the need for good supports and foundations in a building.

In the temple there were many pillars that stood tall and strong. These pillars kept the building from suffering damage and collapsing during calamity. Although this church may have been weak, they were holding on to the promise that there was (and still is) coming a day, after they have come through the difficulties and persecutions, when God would establish them as strong pillars in His temple and they would never be removed!

At the moment there may have been weakness and trembling, but there is coming a day! Claim that word over your life right now! You may be feeling spiritually anemic, worn out, stressed out, burned out, or just down and out, but hold on to what God has spoken to you because there is coming a day when the reward will be greater than the trial!

He will establish you as a strong and mighty article in His presence. The strength you will have as a pillar in the temple of God will far exceed even your greatest moments of strength in this life!

In that time you will stand strong and whole in a glorified body and will never have to worry about sin, persecution, or fear again!

Revelation 3:12 states that here will be three names written upon those who overcome. These names are as follows:

1.) The name of God
2.) The name of the city of God (New Jerusalem)
3.) The new name of the Lord

There is symbolism to each of these names being written upon the believer who has overcome. The name of God upon them signifies that they have been counted worthy to have the right to lay claim to the rewards of God and His presence. This is similar to how a will acknowledges those who will receive the inheritance from the estate.

Because they will be recognized by His name written upon them, they can lay claim to the inheritance in Him that is set before them.

The name of the city of God identifies them as citizens of eternal life. As a birth certificate or passport identifies someone as a citizen of a certain country, so the name of the city of God upon the overcomers will prove their citizenship. They can enjoy all the rights and freedoms that citizenship affords them. They will live and prosper in the city of God!

The new name mentioned in Revelation 3:12 that is written upon the overcomer is the name of the Lord Himself. This name upon the believers will show that they belong to Jesus Christ! It is a new name that He will display on them. It proves ownership much like children write their names on toys or books to show that these belong to them and no other children can claim them. Those who overcome will then belong completely to Jesus Christ and enjoy all the privileges and honors of being heirs of the kingdom of God.

What a great day that will be! Not only will the victorious ones be caught away by the Lord, but we will get to dwell in the city of God and enjoy His presence for all eternity! Until then, we are instructed to hold fast what we have right now in Christ so we don't lose the crown of life! We must cling to it with every last ounce of strength and breath in our bodies, understanding the reward that comes with being faithful to this crown and the penalty for forfeiting it. We must hear what the Spirit is saying to us today!

~

It is God who arms me with strength, And makes my way perfect. He makes my feet like the feet of deer, And sets me on my high places. He teaches my hands to make war, So that my arms can bend a bow of bronze. You have also given me the shield of Your salvation; Your right hand has held me up, Your gentleness has made me great. You enlarged my path under me, So my feet did not slip. I have pursued my enemies and overtaken them; Neither did I turn back again till they were destroyed. I have wounded them, So that they could not rise; They have fallen under my feet. For You have armed me with strength for the battle; You have subdued under me those who rose up against me.

—Psalm 18:32–39 (NKJV)

CHAPTER 8

What's Your Temperature?
The Church of Laodicea

And to the angel of the church of the Laodiceans write, "These things says the Amen, the Faithful and True Witness, the Beginning of the creation of God:'I know your works, that you are neither cold nor hot. I could wish you were cold or hot. So then, because you are lukewarm, and neither cold nor hot, I will vomit you out of My mouth. Because you say, 'I am rich, have become wealthy, and have need of nothing and do not know that you are wretched, miserable, poor, blind, and naked. I counsel you to buy from Me gold refined in the fire, that you may be rich; and white garments, that you may be clothed, that the shame of your nakedness may not be revealed; and anoint your eyes with eye salve, that you may see. As many as I love, I rebuke and chasten. Therefore be zealous and repent. Behold, I stand at the door and knock. If anyone hears My voice and opens the door, I will come in to him and dine with him, and he with Me. To him who overcomes I will grant to sit with Me on My throne, as I also overcame and sat down with My Father on His throne. He who has an ear, let him hear what the Spirit says to the churches.'"

—Revelation 3:14–22 (NKJV)

Laodicea was another city of wealth and prosperity. Banking and trade were big business there. Laodicea was famous for its textiles and wool. "Its school of medicine was known far and wide for its eye salve," according to R. Hollis Gause in his book titled *Revelation: God's Stamp of Sovereignty on History.*

Laodicea was an extremely rich city in which to live. Into this place of resource and affluence came the Word of God to the church in Laodicea. This time there were no commendations or favorable words. There was no applause or praise. There was only rebuke spoken to them by the Lord Himself.

He is identified as the Amen. The meaning of the word *amen* in the Greek is "to be established and sure, to be trustworthy."

Being referred to by this name, the Lord was showing that who He is and what He was about to say was established and trustworthy! Since He was the Amen, naturally He would be a faithful and true witness!

Having watched many court dramas and sitcoms, we realize how important a witness can be. Their true statements can change everything in the courtroom. Their trustworthy assessment of what they saw and what they know can bring freedom to the innocent and conviction to the guilty! And Christ's appraisal of this church is sobering.

He was acknowledged as the beginning of the creation of God. This does not infer that Christ was part of creation or that He was created. Rather this Scripture is saying that Christ was present at the beginning of the creation of God. "In the beginning was the Word and the Word was with God and the Word was God" (John 1:3 NKJV).

He was there in the beginning, and along with the Father and the Spirit spoke the world into existence. He is the first and the last, the Alpha and Omega, the beginning and the end! As such, He has the right to speak these words of accusation against this church.

All of these introductions were to advise the church concerning the identity of the one speaking to them! As mentioned previously, we tend to place value on information we receive based on who is speaking or relaying the information to us. If it is someone we trust, then we will accept it, but if it is someone we don't trust, we will let it go in one ear and out the other!

Although the penmanship in this letter was John's, the words and the inspiration came from a greater and higher authority—the Amen, the true and faithful witness, the beginning of the creation of God.

He declared to Laodicea just as with the other churches that He was fully aware of their deeds. His disapproval of this church was that they were neither hot nor cold but lukewarm. The words *hot* and *cold* speak of two opposite extremes, and in this statement the Savior could have dual meanings.

Laodicea was situated in the Lycus River Valley along with two other cities, one named Hierapolis and the other named Colossae. Hierapolis was a city known for its hot mineral springs, which provided medicinal and therapeutic remedies. This hot water was also used as a cleansing and purifying agent.

The water in Colossae flowed from a cold spring and was very cold and refreshing. It was used to quench thirst and to revitalize.

Laodicea, on the other hand, boasted neither of those things because their water had to be piped in through an aqueduct system, which meant that whether they got their water from the hot mineral springs of Hierapolis or the cold water springs of Colossae, it was lukewarm by the time it reached Laodecia.

The fact was that the water in its lukewarm state was not profitable for therapeutic or medical purposes. Nor was it refreshing.

The first meaning, which is very practical, was that as believers they were neither healing and therapeutic nor cold and refreshing.

A nice hot, relaxing bath when we are not feeling well or when we are stressed out is a beautiful thing!

A nice cold glass of water when we are parched and thirsty brings refreshment and rejuvenation every time!

Since the Laodiceans would comprehend the practical aspects of the difference in water temperatures, it could be the Lord was using this word illustration to show them that they were not fulfilling what was necessary in the body of Christ. They were not healing (hot) physically or spiritually the lives of those around them. Nor were they refreshing and restoring (cold) those who were in need.

Any time we truly enter the presence of God, healing and refreshing take place. No matter what our day or week or month or year has been like, when we kneel at our bed and pray or when we go into our prayer closet and get alone with God, we enter His throne room, His presence. It is there that He will heal our wounded hearts, our secret scars, and our brokenness that no one else may see.

In those moments His Spirit flows in like a river, and even though we may have been burnt out and used up when we walked into His presence, we will leave refreshed, renewed, and whole.

One of the symptoms of not having been in the presence of God is lukewarmness. We try to pipe things into our lives from other sources, thinking they will satisfy. We look for this quick fix or that simple solution. We seek out the warm, fuzzy feelings and the goose-pimple experiences, thinking those things will fulfill, but before we realize what has happened, we are lukewarm.

Nothing that is channeled into our lives through other sources will bring the revival and exhilaration we need. Only when the Spirit of God dwells within us will we find those "rivers of living water flowing out of us" (John 7:38 NKJV).

The Spirit of the Lord will be that spring of water within us that is healing and refreshing us day by day. He is the source and the provider of this water. When this river of His Spirit is flowing from us, we will fulfill His purposes of bringing life and health and refreshment to those around us!

The second meaning is probably the one most of us have heard on numerous occasions where *hot* refers to being completely on fire for God and totally consumed by His Spirit and *cold* represents a coldness of heart and an exhaustive apathy toward the things of God.

In these extremes, lukewarmness would be equal to one who tries to straddle the proverbial fence. That relationship with God is a take-it-or-leave-it kind of thing. At one time these people might have been hot and on fire for God; however, things may have happened, and time may have passed. The fervency may have dwindled until all that was left was a lukewarm, tepid remnant of a Christian.

I love to drink coffee, and when I do, my coffee has to be hot, hot, hot. When I order my caramel macchiato from Starbucks, I ask them to make it extra hot. When I make coffee at home and it finishes brewing and I have filled my cup, I immediately pop it in the microwave to make it even hotter. I can't stand lukewarm or cold coffee. It just makes me gag!

This is how the Lord feels about those who try to live lukewarm, halfhearted existences within His body. He didn't just say, "I will politely spit you out of my mouth." His words have the meaning of "I will wretch and projectile vomit you out of My mouth!" *Gross!* Lukewarmness is nauseating to a holy God, and it should be to us as well! I don't want to make God sick!

Whichever interpretation we take of the temperature issue, the result of neither one is appealing. This was a wake-up call for this church, and it should be for us today. God wants all or nothing from our lives. Do not offer Him that which is lukewarm because it breaks His heart when you do.

As affluent and self-dependent as the church was in Laodicea, take that and double it, and you possibly have the church in America! It is incredulous that with all the resources available to Christians today, all the church doors that are open, all the Christian television programming and networking opportunities we have, we still find ourselves so often in this place of lukewarmness and complacency concerning the things of God.

J. Hampton Keathley, III, says, "America has more churches per capita than any other country. Our currency reads, 'In God We Trust,' but according to recent statistics, there is very little difference between the lifestyles of Christians and non-Christians. The moral degeneracy of our nation in its attitudes, values, and beliefs is everywhere obvious."

In light of this statement, where are those who are healing? Where are those who are refreshing? Where are those who are experiencing the burning revival of a mighty God? Who will keep the rivers of God flowing to those who are hurting and lost?

Don't get me wrong. There are remnants of those who are faithfully seeing miraculous moves of God, and their personal lives are demonstrating the work of the Spirit; however, for the most part the church of today has become so comfortable, prosperous, and self-sufficient that we feel we don't really need God anymore because we can "have church" our own way!

We know how to say the right things, sway crowds with our preaching, and move the masses through our music, but in the process of all this are we simply conduits for a lukewarm stream? In all our intelligence, talent, and opulence, have we allowed the flow of God's Spirit to become ineffective?

The people of the church in Laodicea saw themselves as being rich, wealthy, and in need of nothing. They were completely oblivious that there was even a problem. They thought everything was great and didn't even suspect there was an issue. They were blinded by the things of this world and couldn't see just how far they had strayed from the Lord. They hadn't even missed His presence because of the listless condition of their hearts. Did you catch that?

How sad when the way we perceive ourselves is in such stark contrast to the way God sees us! They thought they were sophisticated, wealthy, and stylish, and the Lord told them they were wretched, miserable, poor, blind, and naked—all the things they didn't want to be, all the things they had no idea they were!

This is the dangerous area of lukewarmness. The place of apathy where we are not even aware there is something separating us from God. It is frightening when our hearts become so calloused we cannot even feel the absence of His presence. If we blindly walk through life and think everything is wonderful because we have some money in the bank, we occasionally go to church, and we are basically good people, then we will one day realize that this is not enough. There is more to our walk with God than having an apathetic attitude, which causes us to just go through the motions without any true passion.

Think about your own pilgrimage with God. What is your spiritual temperature?

You see, the Enemy would love to blind your eyes and have you continue to casually claim the name of Christianity without any fervency or healing or refreshing. The Enemy doesn't care how many times you go to church or how much you put in the offering plate as long as you personally continue to just straddle that fence.

Lukewarmness will steal your relationship with Jesus Christ and your life! Indifference will rob you of the victory that is rightfully yours! Complacency will cause you to be expelled from the mouth of the Lord, and you will find yourself distanced from His presence.

This is what it was doing to the church in Laodicea. The Lord gives them advice on what to do to get rid of this disease of being lukewarm. In Revelation 3:18 (NKJV), He said, "Buy from me gold refined in the fire."

This gold is a symbol of spiritual riches in Christ, a life that has been purified and made complete in the fire, a life that shines with the luminescence of His Spirit, a life that is to be valued and set apart! The lives they were living was a façade, but they could have the real gold. They could be spiritually rich rather than destitute!

Likewise, we must desire the riches of the Spirit of God over anything this earth has to offer. Our commitment and relationship with the Lord is the most necessary thing in life. It is extremely important for us to pay attention to the true condition of our lives in Christ. We must constantly check the water of our spirit for temperature deviations that can lead to lukewarmness. We cannot allow ourselves to become something that is repulsive to the taste buds of God!

"Buy from me white garments that you may be clothed and the shame of your nakedness may not be revealed" (Revelation 3:18). The white garments mentioned in this Scripture were opposite of the fine textiles and black wool, which was a status symbol in Laodicea. These were white garments of holiness, righteousness, and purity. These garments would cover up the shame associated with their sin and lukewarmness.

They would not be able to attain this wardrobe at the neighborhood department store or order it through a Laodicean catalog. The only place they could buy these fine clothes was from Jehovah Himself. He was the designer and Creator of this line of pure white garments. He alone could clothe them to cover up their spiritual nakedness just as He clothed Adam and Eve to hide their physical nakedness. Without His garments they would continue to remain exposed to the elements of their sin and shame!

"Anoint your eyes with eyesalve that you may see" (Revelation 3:18 NKJV). As mentioned earlier in this chapter, Laodicea had cornered the market on medicinal eye salve, but what Christ was speaking of here was not a prescription that comes in a bottle or a tube. His eye salve is a healing for spiritual eyes.

Only when our spiritual eyes are open and healed can we truly see the condition of our hearts and our spirits in the way God sees it. The only way for the people of Laodicea to grasp the concept of how far from God they truly were was to apply the eye salve of the Son of God. The necessity of this is still valid today! There are so many who need to have their spiritual eyes opened to see the true condition of their lives. Our world has become so blinded to the truth of God that we are looking for a remedy in every place but the right place!

Jesus is the Great Physician, and He is the only one authorized to write this prescription! Don't look for it anywhere else. Don't try to find another source or supplier. If you do, you will find yourself with a cheap imitation that will only cause further blindness!

Jesus stated that they were to buy "these things" from Him because this was a city, much like ours, with people who understood consumerism. "These things," however, are of such value that unless He gave them freely to those who ask, we could not afford them.

It has been said that when people are shopping for a luxury item like a Rolls-Royce, if they have to ask the price, then they probably can't afford it. These items the Laodiceans were instructed to buy were far beyond what they could pay. You can't even put a price on what Christ has to offer. It is invaluable!

His desire was to love this church and see them change their ways. He called them to a place of repentance that their eyes would be opened and their lives would be transformed. He wanted them to zealously and passionately turn from the lives they had been living and reap the benefits of the investment they would make in Him!

What will it take for our spiritual eyes to be opened today? In this world where so much tries to blind us from the true spiritual conditions around us, it can be difficult to have our eyes open and see clearly.

It is like trying to keep your eyes wide open when you are in the middle of a sandstorm. Every ounce of self-preservation screams at you to close your eyes so you don't get sand in them because that will hurt, but you know if you close your eyes, you can't see where you are going or how to get out of the sandstorm.

Sadly there are many who have allowed the sandstorms of their lives and of our world to cause them to close their eyes, and they will never see beyond their spiritual eyelids unless they allow the Spirit of God to apply the healing salve.

Jesus told them He was standing at the door and knocking. His longing and desire was to come in and fellowship with whomever opened the door. It wouldn't have mattered if it was one of them or a thousand and one of them. The ones who heard His voice and opened the door would receive the greatest gift and privilege they could ever have.

There are few greater joys than when a friend drops by your house and knocks on the door. We love to have our friends come over. When they knock on the door or ring the doorbell, what do you do? Do you lock the door, turn off the lights, and pretend that no one is home? Maybe there are some people in your life who make you want to do that! When it is a good friend though, you open the door wide and invite that person in. You are hospitable and ask if your friend would like something to drink or eat (or maybe your friend has been to your house enough times that he or she can just open the refrigerator and help him or herself). Then you sit down to talk and share together.

Laugh or cry together. Hang out together and fellowship. This is the response the Lord is wanting when we hear Him knock on the door of our hearts.

Do you hear the knocking of the Savior in your own life today? Do you hear His voice calling out to you? Don't turn away. Don't turn off the lights and pretend no one is home. Go ahead! Answer that door, and your life will never be the same!

He will come in and commune with you. The sorrow you have carried around, He can turn it to joy. The fear that has captured your heart, He will drive it away and give you perfect peace. The shame you have felt because of your failure and sin, He will replace with forgiveness and purpose.

In Revelation 3:21, it says, "To him who overcomes I will grant to sit with Me on My throne, as I also overcame and sat down with My Father on His throne." This is an eternal promise for those who overcome until the end! Jesus Christ is the King of Kings and the Lord of Lords. Just as He overcame this earth, the temptations of this flesh, sin, crucifixion, death, and the grave and now reigns in authority, He has promised that those who overcome will share with Him in this kingdom! We will sit in heavenly places.

We will inhabit His throne room with Him. God the Father rewarded the faithfulness of Jesus Christ by raising Him from the dead and giving Him the name that is above every name. He gave Him power and authority to rule, and we have an opportunity to be a part of that!

He has opened His throne room to us! When we have been faithful, we don't have to shy away from Him, but we can boldly approach His throne. He believes in you so much that He is willing to give you the opportunity to sit with Him on His throne.

I remember times as a child when my dad or my granddad would let me drive the tractor or riding mower with them. I would sit in one of their laps and have my hands on the steering wheel. It was fun and exciting as a child to have the chance to do that, even though Dad's hands were also on the steering wheel and Dad's feet were on the pedals and Dad was still in complete control. At that moment I was able to share the driver's seat with him! God, our Father, will let us share His driver's seat when we have been faithful and have overcome through His Spirit.

How amazing are the promises of God to those who look beyond the riches, styles, and temptations of this temporal world and put on the spirit of an overcomer!

~

But what things were gain to me, these I have counted loss for Christ. Yet indeed I also count all things loss for the excellence of the knowledge of Christ Jesus my Lord, for whom I have suffered the loss of all things, and count them as rubbish, that I may gain Christ and be found in Him, not having my own righteousness, which is from the law, but that which is through faith in Christ, the righteousness which is from God by faith; that I may know Him and the power of His resurrection, and the fellowship of His sufferings, being conformed to His death, if, by any means, I may attain to the resurrection from the dead.

—Philippians 3:7–11 (NKJV)

CHAPTER 9

Can You Hear Me Now?

In each of the letters to the churches in Revelation, the phrase, "He who has an ear, let him hear what the Spirit says to the church," is repeated. Just as the Spirit of the Lord had a word for each of those churches, so He still does for the body of Christ and each of us individually today! We must be careful and attentive to hear what His Spirit is speaking to us.

For those who have experienced hearing loss, you know how difficult it is to be in a restaurant or a public setting where there is a lot of background noise to still hear and hold a conversation. Background noise and other voices tend to fill your ears and distort or completely override the voice of the one to whom you are listening.

It is frustrating, and you get nothing out of the conversation. You find yourself at times answering questions that no one has asked or chiming in with a statement that has nothing to do with the current topic of conversation.

This seems to be how many people live their spiritual lives. At times it's not that they don't want to hear what the Spirit of the Lord is saying. It's just that there is so much background noise and so many other voices and distractions speaking to their lives that they cannot clearly make out the message God is speaking!

If we don't hear clearly and distinctly what the Father is saying, then we will not be able to do what He wants us to do. We will miss his direction and instruction.

For example, if I go to my son's bedroom to tell him to clean his room and he is talking on the phone with his girlfriend while texting another friend and simultaneously Skyping with another friend with loud music playing in the background, the chances of him hearing me and really paying attention to what I am directing him to do are very slim. Trust me on this because I have been run over by this train on many occasions. He doesn't hear exactly what I have said to him, or his brain doesn't process fully my desire because he is distracted by phones and texting and Skyping and music. So when I return later to check on his progress and make sure he has done what I've told him to do and he looks at me with a deer-in-headlights stare, immediately I know he didn't hear and follow through, and immediately he knows I am not pleased.

This is why it is so important for us to have time to get away from all the busyness and noise of our lives to just spend time with the Lord. We need time to just lay our head on His chest and hear His heartbeat without the interference of other things.

We must come to know the voice of our Father and shepherd so we can quickly pick it out from all the other voices and noises that crowd our lives. If we don't, we can't listen intently to Him, and we won't be able to understand or follow through with what He has asked us to do.

Jesus said in John 10 (NKJV), "I am the Good Shepherd, My sheep hear My voice, and I know them, and they follow Me. And I give them eternal life, and they shall never perish; neither shall anyone snatch them out of My hand."

We need to be so familiar with His voice that even if He whispers in the midst of chaos, our ears instantly tune in to Him so that we can acutely discern what He is saying to us and follow Him! If we do not know His voice, we will be distracted by all the other sounds and noises around us and easily become confused.

We will ask ourselves questions like these: "Is this really God speaking to me, or was this just the pizza I ate last night?" "Did the Lord really call me to this, or did my momma call me to this?" "How do I know if this is really God speaking to me?"

Just as I can pick out the voice of my wife in a crowded room and tell by the inflection and intonation of her voice what kind of day she is having, I should also be that familiar with the voice of my Lord and Savior... and even more so!

If a person doesn't hear what the Spirit is saying, they will continue on a path that leads them further and further from Him. They will find themselves walking in confusion and disobedience.

Without the assistance of modern technology I cannot stand in the city I live in and say something and expect someone in the next city to hear what I am saying. Why then do we think we can travel so far away from God and still be able to hear Him?

We must draw near to Him. We must pursue His heart. We must long for His voice. Regardless of what He says, we should just desire to hear from Him. It doesn't matter if He says yes or no or tells us to wait because we just want to hear His voice!

Oh, God, that You would speak clearly to Your servants, open the ears of our understanding and stir our hearts once again! Help us to listen beyond the drone and murmurs of this world.

There is an interesting narrative in the Word of God found in 2 Kings 19. In the previous chapter (18) of this story, the mighty prophet Elijah had just finished with one of the most powerful moves of God in his life when he left Mount Carmel. The prophets of Baal were defeated by a simple prayer and a powerful demonstration of a mighty God.

When Elijah prayed, the fire of God fell from heaven and consumed the sacrifice, the altar, and the water surrounding the altar. It was a huge display of God's power and proof to the nation that Jehovah truly is the living God!

However, instead of celebrating the victory of his God, Elijah was running for his life and hiding away in a cave. The queen, Jezebel, had issued a threat against Elijah because of the events of that day, and it struck fear in his heart.

This is where we pick up the story. In 2 Kings 19:9–13 (NKJV), the Scripture says,

> And there he went into a cave, and spent the night in that place; and behold, the word of the Lord came to him, and He said to him, "What are you doing here, Elijah?" So he said, "I have been very zealous for the Lord God of hosts; for the children of Israel have forsaken Your covenant, torn down Your altars, and killed Your prophets with the sword. I alone am left; and they seek to take my life." Then He said, "Go out, and stand on the mountain before the Lord." And behold, the Lord passed by, and a great and strong wind tore into the mountains and broke the rocks in pieces before the Lord, but the Lord was not in the wind; and after the wind an earthquake, but the Lord was not in the earthquake; and after the earthquake a fire, but the Lord was not in the fire; and after the fire a still small voice. So it was, when Elijah heard it, that he wrapped his face in his mantle and went out and stood in the entrance of the cave. Suddenly a voice came to him, and said, "What are you doing here, Elijah?"

Notice in this passage that the Lord did not speak to Elijah out of the strong wind. He could have, but He didn't. God did not even speak to Elijah through the earthquake. He could have, but He didn't. He refrained from uttering a word to Elijah even when the fire was raging. He could have, but He didn't!

It wasn't until all those things were over that God spoke to him in a "still, small voice" and gave Elijah clear directions! Elijah heard the word of the Lord and was obedient!

I am convinced that many times we need to just be quiet and hear the voice of God! If we would listen and discern His voice and walk in obedience, it would change our lives and change our world!

The church has allowed so much to come in and clog her ears! We must clean out our spiritual ears! Grab a Q-tip and clean out the debris! We must remove the earplugs! We must receive a word and revelation from the Lord for this generation!

If this generation does not hear the words of God and walk in obedience, we can expect it to be more difficult for the generations coming after us to follow God victoriously!

In the military one of the most important ingredients in winning a conflict is communication! If one side knocks out the communication capabilities of their opponent, then it is so much easier for them to gain the upper hand and win the victory! Communication is key in any battle!

In January 1991, then joint chiefs of Staff Chairman Colin Powell, in preparing for Operation Desert Storm against Iraqi forces, stated, "Our strategy to go after this army is very, very simple. First, we're going to cut it off, and then we're going to kill it. To cut it off, that began last week when we started to go after the nerve center, the brains of the operation, the command and control of the operation, and the lines of communication that come out of Baghdad and other places in the country."

As the battle began, American forces first destroyed Iraqi radar and communications systems and then other main elements of the Iraqi antiaircraft network. By doing this, they were able to disconnect the leadership from their forces. This weakened the Iraqi efforts at resistance and fragmented them because they had no clear directives and orders. Ultimately the United States and their allies were able to bring liberty and freedom for Kuwait.

If we can't communicate or can't hear what the commanding officer is saying, we might walk into a trap or into a line of enemy fire! We will find ourselves vulnerable and compromised because there is no clear mandate.

For too long the church has allowed the Enemy to distort and twist the message of the Lord. He has been successful in dulling, deafening, and distracting our ears so we can't hear what the Spirit of God is saying to us. He wants to cut us off from the voice of God and then kill us! We must turn the tables on the Enemy's plan. We must allow the Spirit of God to open our ears, restore those lines of communication, and speak His will!

Hearing what the Spirit is saying is imperative to winning spiritual battles and becoming more than a conqueror through Jesus Christ.

How can we know what to do or what to avoid if we can't hear His voice? Lay down some of the distractions. Turn off the television. Power off your cell phone. Step away from YouTube. Put down the gaming controller. Get away from all the other voices and hear what the Spirit is saying.

So how do we hear His voice? It is simple and probably something we have heard many times before. First and foremost we must get alone with Him in prayer! He is calling us to those moments at His feet.

In His presence He speaks to us. He whispers to us, and He reveals Himself to us!

Isaiah 6 records a time when Isaiah was swept up into the presence of the Lord and He saw the Lord seated on His Throne. God spoke to Isaiah that day in a way Isaiah had never heard God speak before.

In that time with God Isaiah's attention wasn't divided between God and the king and the nation of Israel and his family and his neighbors. He was alone in God's company.

Do you want to hear the voice of the Lord? First, come to His throne room. Lose yourself in His presence. Detach yourself for a season from the crowd. Step away from those close to you who speak into your life. Get alone with God. See Him seated on His throne and listen to Him speak with words that can shake not only the mountains and the earth but can also shake the foundation of your very heart and soul with just His still, small voice.

Secondly we must be in His Word! We must be students of the Bible. The Bible is alive and life-changing. When you begin to read and study the Word of God, ask the Holy Spirit to give you wisdom and understanding.

Don't let your mind be distracted by thinking of everything you have to do when you finish reading the Bible, because you will get nothing out of it! Don't wait until the end of the day when you are exhausted and weary to try to get into the Word of God, because you will be too tired to hear from Him and you will probably fall asleep!

Ask God to speak to you through His written word. When you do this, you will find you grow deeper and stronger. Things will be revealed to your spirit that will mature you and give you the strength to say no to sin and temptation. You will be filled and enabled with the power of the Word of the Lord. His Word is alive, powerful, and effective!

We are to read it, meditate upon it, and write it on the doorposts of our home (or at least on post-it notes you can leave around your home) so that not only are we getting into the Word, but the Word is getting into us as well!

Thirdly we must come together with other believers for worship and teaching or preaching! There is something about being together and connecting with others in the body of Christ that centers us and focuses us on hearing God. The Holy Spirit can use other men and women to speak His Word so we can hear and understand it.

Forget about the things that have kept you from going to church. Dismiss the hurt or rejection you may have experienced in the past. Do not consider those who may be hypocrites in the church because that is between them and God and has nothing to do with you or your relationship to Jesus Christ!

In the church there are true and mature Christians who love the Lord with everything in them. Find them and get to know them because they can be uplifting and encouraging to you in the struggles you deal with. You need the body of Christ in order to be mature and complete!

There is nothing more encouraging than to hear the testimonies of others who have already been through what you are going through and have come out victoriously. They may have retained a few scars as proof of their battle, but they ultimately came out as victors!

When we come together with other believers, our individual and corporate focus should remain on God and God alone. We receive encouragement and refreshing when we come together and God's Word comes forth loud and clear!

~

How can a young man cleanse his way? By taking heed according to Your word. With my whole heart I have sought You; Oh, let me not wander from Your commandments! Your word I have hidden in my heart that I might not sin against You. Blessed are You, O LORD! Teach me Your statutes. With my lips I have declared all the judgments of Your mouth. I have rejoiced in the way of Your testimonies, as much as in all riches. I will meditate on Your precepts, and contemplate Your ways. I will delight myself in Your statutes. I will not forget Your word.

—Psalm 119:9–16 (NKJV)

CHAPTER 10

So... Let's Recap!

In the final analysis of this world and our life experiences, it should not be a surprise to us when we face troubles, persecutions, temptations, difficulties, family problems, financial problems, immorality, undefined issues of right and wrong, idolatry, promiscuity, violence, and more. The Word of God warns us that we will see these things, but that doesn't mean Satan has gained the upper hand and wrestled control away from God. We are promised by Christ in Scripture that we are overcomers in Him.

At times we may question whether or not God is still in control or if He is simply unaware of what is going on or if He just doesn't care. We wonder how God can allow sin and violence to seemingly continue unchecked. We ask questions like these: "Why would God allow this to happen to me?" "Where is God when this abuse is taking place?" "Can God really help me with this because I have been praying for so long and haven't received an answer yet?"

I want you to know today that God is still in control. The things happening around us and in us do not shake Him or cause Him to worry. He still sits on the throne of heaven reigning over all.

He is fully and intimately aware of everything! He is everywhere at the same time. He can give His complete attention and presence to what you are dealing with and at the same time be completely present and involved in what I am going through even though we may be hundreds of miles apart. God is not limited by geography, time, or space.

This concept can be difficult for us to grasp because we can only be in one place at one time and can only give our attention to one thing at a time. Whatever you are going through or struggling with right now, He is there with you just as He is right here with me! God is still alive! God is still powerful! God is still changing lives.

Putting ourselves in the proper position to receive from Him is what we all need to make a priority in our lives. We must strive every day to seek first the kingdom of God and His righteousness, and then all these things (the things we've been praying and believing for) within His will can be given to us in His perfect timing. Maybe we need to change our mind-set. Rather than seeking victory, we should be seeking the God who can give us victory.

When we are pursuing God, He leads us to victory! In our quest for Him, we put ourselves in the right place and posture for the Holy Spirit to come in and strengthen us first, and then triumph is a natural result. Being an overcomer in our spirit man has everything to do with our relationship with God.

George Mueller wrote, "Nine-tenths of the difficulties are overcome when our hearts are ready to do the Lord's will, whatever it may be. When one is truly in this state, it is usually but a little way to the knowledge of what His will is."

Is your heart ready to do God's will no matter what it may require to bring the results?

For Joshua and the children of Israel it meant marching around the walls of Jericho specifically as God had spoken. Then the walls fell.

For Esther it meant praying and fasting and confronting her own fears of entering the presence of the king unannounced. It could have meant her death if the king had desired, but she knew God's Word and decided she would do what needed to be done even if it meant sacrificing her own life. Then she and the Jews were spared and delivered.

Because his heart was right with God, David was able to stand in the face of the giant Goliath even when everyone else was content to hide in their tents. When he did, the giant fell!

How close to victory will your relationship with the Lord lead you? Do you seek Him just enough to get yourself to a place where there is a little relief from the battle and then settle in and get comfortable? Do you only want to follow Him if you can dictate where He will lead you?

The Scripture admonishes us in Proverbs 3:5–6 (NKJV) to "trust in the Lord with all your heart, and lean not on your own understanding. In all your ways acknowledge Him, and He shall direct your paths."

The power of the overcomer *is* most certainly attainable. We must first hear what the Spirit of the Lord is saying and gain a greater understanding of it. Remember what He has spoken to us through the life and the pen of John, the revelator in the letters to the churches in Asia Minor. Open your heart, your mind, and your spirit to the voice of God and let your life be forever changed.

For a more precise understanding, I want to recap what we learned in the previous chapters concerning the seven churches mentioned in Revelation 2 and 3. As we look at these in review, remember that the Lord sees and knows our works, our intentions, and our hearts. Good and bad, there is nothing hidden from Him. In knowing this, if we turn back to Him in complete repentance and surrender, He will forgive and strengthen us! So let's remind ourselves of the messages and steps that will lead us to victory and ultimately to the reward promised to the ones who overcome.

The letter to Ephesus reminds us that if we have forsaken our first love to Christ, we must be honest and acknowledge this fact and come back to Him with humility and repentance, confessing our loss and our sin.

It is imperative we return to this first love in Him. If we want to conquer those things in our lives that battle against us, we must initially have a firm foundation. This comes from a living, active relationship with our Lord and Savior, Jesus Christ.

We can't show up daily and fight the battle unless we are fighting it on solid ground! It would be like trying to reach the sky while standing on quicksand! It can't be done!

This could well be what Edward Mote had in mind in 1834 when he penned the following words:

> My hope is built on nothing less
> than Jesus blood and righteousness.
> I dare not trust the sweetest frame,
> But wholly lean on Jesus' name.
>
> On Christ the solid rock I stand.
> All other ground is sinking sand.
> All other ground is sinking sand.

This is the only way we can experience triumph and reap the rewards of eternal life, which He has promised to those who overcome. We must stop showing up for the battle unprepared because we will lose every time.

Through the love of Jesus Christ working in us, there is no defeat, only victory. We may have momentary setbacks; however, His love will see us through those, and we will continue to walk as victors! We don't have to win every small battle in order to win the war, but we do have to show up in order to prevail! When we overcome and eat of the Tree of Life, we will live eternally with Him in victory!

The letter to Smyrna brings clarity to the differences between God's economy and man's economy. We must not judge our spiritual standing by what we have or don't have. We can't determine our blessings by the situations that are currently surrounding our lives. We are blessed even when we are in the middle of a battle.

Some of the most anointed men and women who have ever lived had very little of this world's goods. The reason for this is because they didn't set their sights on obtaining and holding on to temporary things such as money and possessions. They were looking to invest in things that rust cannot destroy, time and elements cannot decay, and moths and bugs cannot consume! Their treasures were being deposited and stored in eternal things!

When our eyes are fixed on eternity, we will have no fear. Persecution can come and try to kick down the wall of faith within us, but fear is no match for faith.

Lack can be so oppressive as to try to steal our joy and cause us to fear what will happen to us and how we are going to survive, but the provision of God is sufficient for all our tomorrows!

The Enemy may level one weapon of warfare after another against us, but the shield of faith will block everyone! Fear is a tool the Enemy uses to try to stop the plan of God in the people of God, but remember, "We have not been given a spirit of fear" (2 Timothy 1:7 NKJV).

God will uncover before our eyes the plans and traps the Enemy has laid for our destruction. He will unwrap before us the strategies that have been leveled against us for our demise! He will tell us the secrets of the Enemy!

When we know what the Enemy's plans are, then we are able to discern at face value the situations we are going through, and we become aware of God's plan for our victory.

In other words, when God reveals to me what is going on and I can see through spiritual eyes, I am no longer questioning and wondering why I am going through this.

In this place I gain a deeper understanding. I can see why I am dealing with this and how God wants to bring me to victory.

Often we find ourselves questioning and doubting when tough times appear, and this leads us to fear. Instead of becoming fearful, we should be praying that God will give us insight into the intel of the Enemy so that even in the middle of the conflict we can understand and know there is a way to conquer.

The words the Spirit spoke to this church were "Be faithful!" I cannot overemphasize this! Faithfulness is so necessary in the lives of believers if they want to see success.

If we are wishy-washy, we will never win. We cannot have victory tomorrow if we are compromising today! We cannot expect God to continually empower us if we are consistently giving in to the temptations before us.

If we surrender to the attacks of the Enemy and allow persecution or fear to stop us, then we become POWs rather than victors. We must strive to walk in faithfulness in everything we do.

We cannot compromise our faithfulness and then blame God when we don't see victory. If God cannot trust us in today's battle, then how can we expect Him to bring us tomorrow's victory?

Mother Teresa of Calcutta is quoted as saying, "I do not pray for success, I ask for faithfulness."

Faithfulness will not always be easy, but it will always bring reward with it! When Christ returns to this earth, He will be looking for faithfulness. He has promised that when we are faithful and we hold fast those things we know to be right and true, then we will not have to be concerned about the second death. It will have no power over us! We will live eternally in the presence of the one who loved us and gave Himself for us! There is no greater reward than this. The treasures of this earth cannot even begin to compare with the compensation the faithful will receive.

The letter to Pergamos reminds us that we must be so careful to shun compromise and continue to win in the small issues of life so that we will not allow inaccurate philosophies and false ideas to shape our beliefs.

Tolerance is a great ideology and should be a part of every Christian's life to an extent. However, I believe we must draw a line in the sand when tolerance brings us to a place of compromising the truth!

We can love those who believe differently than we do, but this does not mean we have to condone or embrace everything they do and believe. Instead, we should speak the truth in love, showing them the love of Jesus, which will influence them far more than words of condemnation.

We must hold on to what we know to be true and right according to God's Word and never let it be removed from our hearts and minds. The psalmist declared, "Your Word, (speaking to God), I have hidden in my heart that I might not sin against You" (Psalm 119:11 NKJV).

If we want to stay true and keep ourselves from thoughts and actions that displease God, then we must keep His Word at the forefront of our hearts and minds! This is the only way we will be able to discern the truth from a lie!

When truth stands as the bouncer at the door of our hearts, deception will be denied entrance to our lives!

The path to true and lasting victory is to utilize the Word of God in this walk of faith. Without His Word being a daily part of our lives and thoughts, we leave ourselves vulnerable and exposed to whatever lies the Devil wants to speak into our minds.

Use God's Word. Speak His Word into your situations, your circumstances, your battles, your difficulties, and your temptations. You will find that the strength of the Lord will arise within you. Your perspective of the struggle will change as you begin to see things through the eyes of the Spirit.

God's ability is not limited by your situations. His Word is powerful and effective and moves like a two-edged sword.

If we are to be delivered from the judgment of God, the only avenue is through repentance! Repentance seems to be a thread that weaves its way through every one of these letters in Revelation.

Repentance is a calling to turn around and come back to the foundational things, which are righteous and holy. God is not interested in how well we can play church or how holy of a facade we can manufacture! He wants our hearts running to Him in surrender and true sorrow. When we respond to Him in this way, He will give us the greatest freedom we have ever known—a freedom of acquittal, a white stone of acceptance and eternal life!

Being a connoisseur of courtroom dramas, I love the moment when someone who is truly innocent receives the verdict of not guilty. You can feel the weight lift in the courtroom. You can see the gratitude in the eyes of the defendant. The whole atmosphere changes because of the relief of freedom!

Not long ago there was a news story playing out on the world stage involving an American student in Italy named Amanda Knox. Having been accused, arrested, and originally convicted in the first level of trial along with her boyfriend for the murder of her roommate, she waited in prison for her appeal in the second phase of her trial. In this second level of trial her conviction was overturned, and she was found innocent of the charges against her.

While people were waiting for this verdict, everyone watching throughout the world held their breath and sat on the edge of their seats. When the verdict of not guilty was announced, there seemed to be a collective sigh of relief because this young lady who previously was found guilty would now be set free and returned to the United States.

How much more exuberance and celebration is there when a lost sinner comes in repentance and receives the greatest acquittal of all time in the heavenly courtroom? All of heaven waits on the edge of their seats, holding their breath and waiting for the moment of declaration. Not guilty! The handcuffs are taken off. The prison doors are opened. The shackles of sin fall away, and they walk into liberty!

The Letter to Thyatira tells us we must commit ourselves to what God has called us to become and to do. Follow-through in matters of the kingdom of God is vitally important. How many battles have not been won because believers have retreated rather than fought? How many miracles have we not experienced because we have given up too soon? How many healings have we forfeited because we have not persevered? How many harvests have not been reaped because the laborers have given up and quit? How many souls have not come into relationship with Jesus Christ because the body of Christ has retreated from the commission set before us?

We must stand firm in what we know to be true and right according to the principles of God's Word. We cannot afford to be swayed or mislead. This is His message to us! Start strong, persevere, and finish stronger!

We must clutch the truth and hold on to it regardless of the cost. We cannot barter, trade, or exchange it for anything! If we do, we walk straight into deception.

Some people may say that we live in an enlightened age. They may say the Bible and the truths contained in it are outdated and antiquated. But I want you to know that the words of God are timeless. His truths are eternal.

These truths were relevant, true, and life-changing for the men who wrote them. They were relevant, true, and life-changing for our ancestors. Today they are relevant, true, and life-changing for us. And likewise, they will be relevant, true, and life-changing for the generations who will follow us. The absolute truth of God's Word is not a lost cause!

Styles may come in and go out, but the Word of God is always relevant. Philosophies and beliefs may change over time, but God's Word is always the same and constant. Rulers and leaders may take office and leave office, but the power of God's Word will always abide in the hearts of men and women.

We should keep ourselves pure before God in body, mind, heart, soul, and spirit.

We must remember that the Lord Jesus Christ paid a high price to redeem us from the curse of sin. Therefore, because He took our place on Calvary to redeem us from the penalty of our sins, He now owns the rights and title to our lives. It is only fitting then to live our lives in a way that is pleasing to Him.

His desire is to transform our spirits, minds, and bodies and for us to be holy. When we are sanctified and living holy lives, there are blessings and rewards that accompany that lifestyle. When we choose not to live righteous lives before the Lord, we must also understand that there are undesirable consequences to our choices that lead to spiritual death.

When we overcome in this life and forsake the things that will corrupt the body and spirit, we are promised that we will reign with Him, and as the Morning Star, He will light the path before us.

The apostle Paul confirms this in 2 Corinthians 7:1 (NKJV) when he writes, "Therefore, having these promises, beloved, let us cleanse ourselves from all filthiness of the flesh and spirit, perfecting holiness in the fear of God."

As Ephesians 6:11–18 (NKJV) reminds us, we must equip ourselves for this pursuit of holiness!

> Finally, my brethren, be strong in the Lord and in the power of His might. Put on the whole armor of God, that you may be able to stand against the wiles of the devil. For we do not wrestle against flesh and blood, but against principalities, against powers, against the rulers of the darkness of this age, against spiritual hosts of wickedness in the heavenly places. Therefore take up the whole armor of God, that you may be able to withstand in the evil day, and having done all, to stand. Stand therefore, having girded your waist with truth, having put on the breastplate of righteousness, and having shod your feet with the preparation of the gospel of peace; above all, taking the shield of faith with which you will be able to quench all the fiery darts of the wicked one. And take the helmet of salvation, and the sword of the Spirit, which is the word of God; praying always with all prayer and supplication in the Spirit, being watchful to this end with all perseverance and supplication for all the saints.

When we put on the full armor of God and walk in the spirit of an overcomer, there is a release from further burden, and we are given the authority and power of Christ. When we overcome, He will be our Morning Star and light the way before us!

The letter to Sardis was written to a church who had a reputation of being alive, but they were dead. What they looked like on the outside was more important to them than what was happening on the inside.

What is the reputation of your life as a Christian? Are you living up to and fulfilling that reputation? If not, why not?

We cannot live in the anointing and presence of God right now if we are holding on to our reputation from the past. How can we grab hold of what God has for us today if our hands are too busy trying to hold on to what we were blessed with yesterday?

Will reputation be an architect and builder in your life, or will it be a demolition crew? Choices we make and the actions and words that accompany those decisions will formulate an opinion in the minds of others about who and what we are. What is the reputation you want the world to see in your life? What is the reputation you want God to see in your life?

Don't allow what used to be alive and vibrant in you to now become nothing more than an extinguished fire and a decaying corpse.

Trying to maintain life in a place of death is impossible and will lead to frustration and defeat! It is time for the church to check her pulse and see if there is still life!

Become one of those few who have not succumbed to death and who still see the need for revival and hear the Spirit call you back to life and strength in Him.

Let the valley that once spoke of the Enemy's power of death and destruction in your life now become an amazing confirmation of God's life-giving power.

When we walk as overcomers in God and do not allow ourselves to become corrupted with the things of this world, then this faith is accounted to us as righteousness, and it makes us worthy through His Spirit to be numbered with the ones who will wear white on that day.

We will walk in white clothing of holiness, righteousness, and purity! There has never been anything on this earth designed and sewn that can rival the garments our Lord and Savior will place upon those who overcome!

We will stand before the throne of God in full assurance and confidence that when He looks in the Book of Life, He will see our names! Our names will forever be written and sealed in the Lamb's Book of Life! What a promise! What a Savior!

The letter to Philadelphia imparted the truth that to live as overcomers, we must know and believe that Jesus Christ is in complete control! He was God in the beginning, and He will be God in the end! He alone holds the key of success in our daily walk of victory! Only He should have the ultimate authority and access to our hearts and lives!

There are times when He may close a door just as we are about to walk through it. If He does, we cannot stand there and bang on the door, demanding that He open it so that we can have our own way! We must trust Him and look for the pathway He is opening before us!

I read an anonymous quote the other day that said, "Until God opens the next door before you, just praise Him in the hallway while you wait!"

Sometimes we can't mount up with wings as eagles and soar because instead of waiting on Him, we are trying to kick the door, which we know He has closed, off its hinges.

What doors has God opened in your life, and what doors has He shut? Don't consider the difficulty or the ease of walking through the door He has opened. Just know that God will give you strength for the journey. You may be tired and weary, but in those moments His strength is made perfect in you if you will only look to Him.

Let faith and trust be part of the process. Ask yourself, "Am I going to trust God even though I don't understand why He has closed this door and opened another? Am I going to have faith in Him even though He answered my prayer in a way I didn't envision?"

Don't let the battles in your life, the closed doors, or the problems you face command what your response will be. Lift up your banner of faith and press through to victory!

There is spiritual warfare going on. Satan is pulling out every trick he can to silence those who proclaim the name of Jesus Christ and to exhaust them of their strength. Nevertheless, I also see and know that God is opening doors to those who have been obedient to Him. He will be faithful to you!

We must embrace the name of Jesus Christ even in a world that detests it. It is critical for us to be willing to hear the Word of the Lord and live in obedience to it even in a world filled with distractions and voices demanding our attention.

Jesus is coming soon, and He is looking for faith and faithfulness.

In the end, He will raise the faithful ones up and make a way of escape. He will install them as a foundational pillar in His eternal temple. He will write upon them His own name (they will be considered worthy to be His heir) and the name of His city (they will be citizen of His heaven) and a new name that only He knows and can give (they will belong completely to Him).

The letter to Laodicea was a stern word for this church that God despises mediocrity. He would rather have us hot or cold, one of the two extremes, than for us to remain undistinguished and indifferent.

This church was not *hot* (bringing healing physically or spiritually to the lives of those around them). Nor were they *cold* (refreshing and restoring those who were in need.)

Their lack of commitment in their relationship with God had caused them to cease fulfilling the purpose for which they had been called!

This was a wake-up call for this church, and it should be for us today. God wants all or nothing from us every single day. We bring sickness to the body of Christ when we choose to live beneath the level of life He purchased for us with His sacrifice on the cross.

Thankfully He wasn't undecided in His commitment to us when He went to Calvary, and we shouldn't be indecisive in our commitment of complete surrender to Him!

The church in Laodicea saw themselves as being rich, wealthy, and in need of nothing. They were completely oblivious that there was even a problem. What a tragedy that plays itself out even still today in so many churches and individuals!

Lukewarmness will steal our relationship with Jesus Christ and our eternal life! Indifference will rob us of the victory that is rightfully ours! Complacency will cause us to be expelled from the mouth of the Lord, and we will find ourselves distanced from His presence.

This is what it was doing to the church in Laodicea. Don't let it happen to you! See yourself through the eyes of the Spirit of God.

The challenge extended to us in this letter is to buy from the Lord gold refined in the fire, that we may be rich; and white garments, that we may be clothed, that the shame of our nakedness may not be revealed; and to anoint our eyes with eye salve, that we may see. These things only come from the Lord! We must hear the rebuke and call of the Lord and quickly repent. Then we will be able to grasp the prize that has been set before us.

What is this valuable prize?

Christ has promised that those who overcome will share with Him in His kingdom! We will sit together with Him in heavenly places.

CHAPTER 11

That's It in a Nutshell!

When my children were young, we loved playing the "Disney Scene It?" game challenge where the picture appears on the screen a little bit at a time and the first one to guess what the picture is or who the character in the scene is wins that round.

In our lives we just see one little bit at a time of the whole picture. When we just see the small fragments of the picture, it is tough to understand what is happening, so we frequently question God's decisions and will.

We see the divided parts and colors, but we don't see the whole tapestry of our lives like God does.

There is coming a day when it will all be revealed to us. The moment we look into the face of Jesus Christ, we will immediately understand. We will have an aha moment. We will say, "Now I get it! Now I understand! All of those things I questioned and doubted now make sense when I see it in His eyes! All those battles I had to fight my way through now I get it!"

We must set our hearts each day on victorious living! We must not become weary in well doing! No more excuses! No more justifications as to why we can't do it today! No more whining and whimpering!

There must still be a remnant of people in this world who are not afraid to stand up to the Enemy, the victory thief, and tell him, "No more!

There has to be a person who will look the Devil in the eye and tell him, "You can't have my focus. You can't have my love for Christ. You can't have my purity. You can't have my thought life. You can't have my family. You can't have what belongs to me. These are the promises of God for my life, and I would rather die than surrender them to anyone!"

My prayer is this: "Lord, please let there be people who will square their shoulders and point their fingers at Satan and say with power and conviction, 'This is what God promised me and blessed me with (victory, strength, love, joy, forgiveness or whatever it may be) and you cannot take it from me!'"

We are not fighting *for* a place of victory, but because of Christ's redemptive work on the cross and the power of the Holy Spirit, we are fighting *from* a place of victory. The victory has already been won, but we must receive it, live it, and walk in it!

The winner takes all!

Jesus was the best example of overcoming we could ever have. He faced a change in form and nature when He laid aside the heavenly and put on His earthly body. He went through the same struggles that we face every day—temptation, anger, fear, weakness, exhaustion, lack of peace, rejection by both enemies and friends, and pain in His body.

He dealt with walking in the ominous shadow of the cross and the anxiety and stress of what would happen. He even prayed in the garden, "Father, if there be any other way, let this cup pass from me!"

This sounds like the words of a man who would rather not face what He was going to have to face, yet He prayed, "Not my will but Your will, Father, be done."

Everything in His fleshly, earthly body screamed out, "I don't want to do this." He knew the pain and anguish that lay before Him, and His humanity cried out for another way! There was a battle waging in His life between His flesh and His spirit! Yet knowing in His spirit the plan of the Father and what the fulfillment of that plan meant for all of us, He bowed to the Father's will and surrendered Himself as a sacrifice for the sins of all mankind.

In that moment, even though His life was being eclipsed by death, He became victorious. God did not remove Him from the situation, but instead God strengthened Him for the task that lay before Him.

We would rather that God just remove us from difficulty so we would not have to face it and could live our lives in comfort, but we need to understand that often God's will may take us to places we would rather not be. This doesn't mean that He has forsaken us. It simply means He is fulfilling His plan in us!

As the church, which is to be the bride of Christ, we must rise up, shake off our complacency, and fix our eyes on Jesus. He is the author and the finisher of our faith, the Savior of our souls, the lover of our lives, our Redeemer, King, and coming groom.

The principle theme in each of these letters in Revelation seems to be repentance and returning to God as the key that unlocks the door of victory. When Israel was in Egyptian bondage, God did not raise up a deliverer until the nation of Israel repented and returned to God's ways. God was still with them even in the land of Egypt, but it wasn't until they repented and cried out to God that He provided a way of escape.

To see victory, be overcomers, and successfully complete the race set before us, we must walk in true repentance, humility, purity, and power. We must understand that it's not by our might and not by our strength but by God's spirit that we overcome!

~

These things I have spoken to you, that in Me you may
have peace. In the world you will have tribulation; but
be of good cheer, I have overcome the world.

—John 16:33 (NKJV)

~

And they overcame him by the blood of the Lamb and by the word
of their testimony, and they did not love their lives to the death.

—Revelation 12:11 (NKJV)

Afterword

This book is a message God spoke into my heart one day during my prayer time. He allowed it to sit and marinate in my spirit for about eight years before He allowed me to write it. Through much prayer, study, and preparation my hope is that, through this book, the heart of God will be seen, the voice of God will be heard, and many lives will be changed. It is my desire that the words contained in this book will strengthen, renew, revive, and move the church forward in this generation.

About the Author

J. C. Weeks graduated from Lee University and has served in ministry for more than twenty-two years. He is the lead pastor of Crossroads Community Church in Titusville, Florida, where he lives with his wife, Melinda, and his son, Jordan. His daughter, Lauren, and son-in-law, Matt, also live in Florida.

Keep showing up every day and keep winning the small battles because the winner takes all!

Printed in the United States
By Bookmasters